Also by
HUNTER LEWIS

ARE THE RICH NECESSARY?

"Highly provocative and highly pleasurable."

—**HARRY HURT III**, *New York Times*

"Great reading."

—*Publishers Weekly*

"Worth reading aloud on a family vacation."

—**GENE EPSTEIN,** *Barron's*

A *Library Journal*
BEST BUSINESS BOOK OF THE YEAR

WHERE KEYNES WENT WRONG

"This wonderful book . . . restores clear thinking and common sense to their rightful places in the economic policy debate."

—**JAMES GRANT, Editor,** *Grant's Interest Rate Observer*

"[A] much needed book.

—**GENE EPSTEIN,** *Barron's*

"Lewis has exposed with unmatched clarity . . . Keynes's system. . . . [This] book is an ideal guide. . . . "

—**DAVID GORDON,** LewRockwell.com

A QUESTION OF VALUES

"An important book."

—HENRY ROSOVSKY, former Dean of Arts and Sciences and currently Lewis P. and Linda L. Geyser University Professor Emeritus, Harvard University

"Enormously worthwhile. . . . provides a unique way of organizing our thinking about values."

—ADELE SIMMONS, President, MacArthur Foundation

"A stimulating book if ever there was one . . . an eye opener."

—DOROTHY B. and HOMER A. THOMPSON, Institute for Advanced Study, Princeton, New Jersey

"Especially useful . . . to help students . . . in actual human decision-making."

—HARVEY COX, Professor of Divinity, Harvard University, and author of *Many Mansions and The Secular City*

Economics in Three Lessons &
One Hundred Economic Laws

Economics in Three Lessons

&

One Hundred Economic Laws

Hunter Lewis

Axios Press
PO Box 457
Edinburg, VA 22824
888.542.9467   info@axiosinstitute.org

Economics in Three Lessons & One Hundred Economic Laws © 2017 by
Axios Press.

Library of Congress Cataloging-in-Publication Data

Names: Lewis, Hunter, author.
Title: Economics in three lessons & one hundred economic laws / Hunter
Lewis.
Other titles: Economics in three lessons and one hundred economic laws
Description: Edinburg, VA : Axios Press, 2017. | Includes bibliographical
references and index.
Identifiers: LCCN 2017021600 | ISBN 9781604191141 (hardcover)
Subjects: LCSH: Economics.
Classification: LCC HB71 .L5463 2017 | DDC 330--dc23 LC record available
at https://lccn.loc.gov/2017021600.

Contents

Economics in Three Lessons

One Hundred Economic Laws

Economics in Three Lessons

[The] suffering [of poverty] is unnecessary because over the centuries a [market] system has been worked out to create "the wealth of nations"—all nations. To bring that system to all the world's poor is . . . our chief unfinished business.[1]

—Michael Novak
1933–2017

Lesson One

Sustainability

Chapter One

Henry Hazlitt's
Invaluable Insight

MOST OF US would agree that the principal difference between children and real adults is that the latter look ahead, consider consequences, act responsibly and sustainably.

Sustainability is not, however, just the essence of maturity. It is, in addition, the essence of logic and of economics. Economics in the final analysis is grounded in logic. Good economics is always logical, which means that it is clear, orderly, organized, relevant, complete, consistent, and above all sustainable.

Economics is not directly about morality. But logic, economics, and the concept of sustainability have much to teach us about morality as well. In his book, *Moral Foundations*, the ornithologist, naturalist, and philosopher Alexander Skutch observed that:

> People . . . might tell us that . . . morality . . . is not lying, not stealing, not killing, not coveting, not cheating, [not] . . . injuring one's neighbor. If asked what common feature unites all these interdicted activities, they would find it difficult to answer. They might say that all these forbidden activities cause people pain. . . . This is true enough, but . . . competition in trade or the professions brings much loss and sorrow to those who fail in it; . . . the punishment of children makes them unhappy; and the practice of medicine and dentistry are abundant sources of pain even to those who ultimately benefit. . . . The common feature which unites the activities most consistently forbidden by the moral codes of civilized peoples is that by their very nature they cannot be both habitual and enduring, because they tend to destroy the conditions which make them possible.[2]

Sustainability is not only the essence of maturity, logic, economics, and morality. It is also the foundation for human happiness. As the ancient Greek philosopher Epicurus wrote:

The . . . chief good is care in avoiding undesired consequences. Such prudence is more precious than philosophy itself, for all the other virtues spring from it. It teaches that it is impossible to live pleasurably without also living prudently, honestly, and justly; [nor is it possible to lead a life of prudence, honor, and justice] and not live pleasantly. For the virtues are closely associated with the pleasant life, and the pleasant life cannot be separated from them.

By far the best treatment of the theme of sustainability in economics is found in Henry Hazlitt's masterpiece, *Economics in One Lesson*, a book published in 1946 that became a surprising best seller and that continues to instruct to this day. Hazlitt introduces his book as follows:

This book is an analysis of economic fallacies that . . . have . . . become a new orthodoxy . . . [despite] their own self-contradictions. . . . There is not a major government in the world at this moment . . . whose economic policies are not influenced, if they are not almost wholly determined, by acceptance of some of these fallacies. Perhaps the shortest and surest way to an understanding of economics is through a dissection of such errors, and particularly of the central error from which they stem.

He then continues in the book itself:

[That] economics is haunted by more fallacies than any other study known to man . . . is no accident. The inherent difficulties of the subject would be great enough in any case, but they are multiplied a thousand fold by . . . the special pleading of selfish interests. . . . While certain public policies would in the long run benefit everybody, other policies would benefit one group only at the expense of all other groups. The group that would benefit by such policies, having such a direct interest in them, will argue for them plausibly and persistently. It will hire the best buyable minds to devote their whole time to presenting its case. And it will finally either convince the general public that its case is sound, or so befuddle it that clear thinking on the subject becomes next to impossible.

In addition to these endless pleadings of self-interest, there is a second main factor that spawns new economic fallacies every day. This is the persistent tendency of men to see only the immediate effects of a given policy, or its effects only on a special group, and to neglect to inquire what the long-run effects of that policy will be not only on that special group but on all groups. It is the fallacy of overlooking secondary consequences.

In this lies almost the whole difference between good economics and bad. The bad economist sees only what immediately strikes the eye; the good economist also looks beyond. The bad economist sees only the direct consequences of a proposed course; the good economist looks also at the longer and indirect consequences. The bad economist sees only what the effect of a given policy has been or will be on one particular group; the good economist inquires also what the effect of the policy will be on all groups.

The distinction may seem obvious.... Doesn't every little boy know that if he eats enough candy he will get sick? ... Do not the idler and the spendthrift know, even in the midst of their glorious fling, that they are heading for a future of debt and poverty?

Yet when we enter the field of public economics, these elementary truths are ignored. There are men regarded today as brilliant economists who deprecate saving and recommend squandering on a national scale as the way of economic salvation; and when anyone points to what the consequences of these policies will be in the long run, they reply flippantly, as might the prodigal son of a warning father: "In the long run, we are all dead." And such shallow wisecracks pass as devastating epigrams and the ripest wisdom.

But the tragedy is that, on the contrary, we are already suffering the long-run consequences of the policies of the remote or recent past. Today is already the tomorrow which the bad economist yesterday urged us to ignore. The long-run consequences of some economic policies may become evident in a few months. Others may not become evident for several years. Still others may not become evident for decades. But in every case, those long-run consequences are contained in the policy as surely as the hen was in the egg, the flower in the seed.

From this aspect, therefore, the whole of economics can be reduced to a single lesson, and that lesson can be reduced to a single sentence. The art of economics consists in looking not merely at the immediate but at the longer effects of any act or policy; it consists in tracing the consequences of that policy not merely for one group but for all groups. . . .

It is true, of course, that the opposite error is possible. In considering a policy, we ought not to concentrate only on its long-run results to the community as a whole. This is the error often made by the classical economists. It resulted in a certain callousness toward the fate of groups that were immediately hurt by policies. . . .

But comparatively few people today make this error. . . . The most frequent fallacy by far today, the fallacy that emerges again and again in nearly every conversation that touches on economic affairs, the error of a thousand political speeches, the central sophism of the "new" economics, is to concentrate on the short-run effects of policies on special groups and to ignore or belittle the long-run effects on the community as a whole.

We have stated the nature of the lesson, and of the fallacies that stand in its way, in abstract terms. But the lesson will not be driven home, and the fallacies will continue to go unrecognized, unless both are illustrated by examples. . . .

There is no more persistent and influential faith in the world today than the faith in government spending. Everywhere government spending is presented as a panacea for all our economic ills. . . . Is there unemployment? That is obviously due to "insufficient private purchasing power." The remedy is just as obvious. All that is necessary is for the government to spend enough to make up the "deficiency."

An enormous literature is based on this fallacy, and, as so often happens with doctrines of this sort, it has become part of an intricate network of fallacies that mutually support each other. We cannot explore that whole network at this point. . . . But we can examine here the mother fallacy that has given birth to this progeny, the main stem of the network. . . .

A certain amount of public spending is necessary to perform essential government functions. A certain amount of public works— of streets and roads and bridges and tunnels, of armories and navy yards, of buildings to house legislatures, police, and fire departments—is necessary to supply essential public services. With such public works, necessary for their own sake, and defended on that ground alone, I am not here concerned. I am here concerned with public works considered as a means of "providing employment" or of adding wealth to the community that it would not otherwise have had.

A bridge is built. If it is built to meet an insistent public demand, if it solves a traffic problem or a transportation problem otherwise insoluble, if, in short, it is even more necessary than the things for which the taxpayers would have spent their money if it had not been taxed away from them, there can be no objection. But . . . for every dollar that is spent on the bridge, a dollar will be taken away from taxpayers. . . . [Whatever] the bridge costs . . . the taxpayers will lose. . . . They will have that much taken away from them which they would otherwise have spent on the things they needed most.

Therefore for every public job created by the bridge project, a private job has been destroyed somewhere else. We can see the men employed on the bridge. We can watch them at work. The employment argument of the government spenders becomes vivid, and probably for most people convincing.

But there are other things that we do not
see, because, alas, they have never been permitted to come into existence. They are the
jobs destroyed by the . . . [funds] taken from
the taxpayers. All that has happened, at best,
is that there has been a diversion of jobs because of the project. More bridge builders;
fewer automobile workers, radio techni-
cians, clothing workers, farmers. . . . What
has happened is merely that one thing has
been created instead of others. . . .

I have deliberately chosen the most favorable
example . . . [from among] public spending
schemes. . . . I have not spoken of the hun-
dreds of boondoggling projects that are invariably embarked upon the moment the
main object is to "give jobs" and "to put
people to work. . . ." It is highly improbable
that the projects thought up by the bureau-
crats will provide the same net addition to
wealth and welfare, per dollar expended, as
would have been provided by the taxpayers themselves, if they had been individu-
ally permitted to buy or have made what
they themselves wanted, instead of being
forced to surrender part of their earnings
to the state. . . .[3]

The lead character in the film *The Big Short*, about the Crash of 2008, says simply that "Short-term thinking and fraud do not work." In saying this, he was echoing Hazlitt.

Lesson Two

The Free Price System[*]

Chapter Two

The Central Role Played by Free Prices

[Soviet] socialism collapsed because it did not tell the economic truth.

—Oystein Dahle[4]

WHY IS THE human race so poor? Why do billions still lack enough even to eat? As this author noted in an earlier book, even a small sum of money, such as $10, if compounded at 3% over 1,000 years, would produce a sum equal to twice the world's wealth today. It should be ridiculously easy, over time, to end human poverty. Why have we failed to do so?

Failure to cooperate, to work together is the obvious answer. There is very little each of us can do alone, but there is endless opportunity in organizing ourselves to work constructively together in an ever broadening circle. Like children, we refuse to do what is clearly in our long-term interest to do. We either think only of the short term, or sacrifice the common and greater good for the immediate benefit of our particular group. Moreover, we cover up and lie about what we are doing, lie both to ourselves and others.

How can we do better? First of all, we must be assured of our physical safety and the safety of our property. How can we consider the long term if our life and property are at risk at any moment from human predators, whether criminal or sanctioned by government? It is difficult to consider the long term if everything we have can be stolen at any moment. But safety and protection from theft is not enough either. In addition, we need an honest system of mutual exchange that everyone can rely on. A corrupt and dishonest economic system does not create wealth; it destroys it.

The most reliable barometer of economic honesty is to be found in prices. Honest prices, neither manipulated nor controlled, provide both investors and consumers with reliable economic signals. They show, beyond any doubt, what is scarce, what is plentiful, where opportunities lie, and where they do not lie.

A corrupt economic system does not want honest prices, honest information, or honest results. The truth may be inconvenient or unprofitable for powerful government leaders or private interests allied with them. Typically, throughout human history, these leaders and special interests have sought to use their power to manipulate and control prices to their own advantage.

Much of the time, powerful price manipulators and controllers are accompanied and assisted by ideologists or theoreticians, special pleaders for hire, as described by Hazlitt. These professional advisors—skilled verbally or in mathematics—confidently argue that dishonest prices are really honest; honest prices are really dishonest; the resulting chaos is really order; and a future filled with jobs and plenty lies ahead with just a few more manipulations or controls. Sometimes the arguments are presented with calculated deceit, sometimes with muddled sincerity.

Can it really be this simple, that job growth and economic prosperity will follow if we provide a safe environment and allow economic prices to tell the truth, free from the self-dealing and self-interested theories of powerful special interests? That is the central thesis of this lesson, and each chapter will explore it from an additional angle. What is needed to pull humanity out of dire poverty is a free price system, one that is neither manipulated nor controlled.

If prices are not free, an economic system cannot be expected to function properly. What happens thereafter will depend on the degree of price manipulation or control. If it is not extreme, the economy may limp along, impaired, not realizing its full potential, but not in overt crisis.

If the undermining of free prices is extreme enough, the system will visibly falter and may even collapse, as in 1929 or 2008. In this case, capital, jobs, and people's lives are destroyed. Ironically, the crisis often leads to a government response entailing even more price manipulation or control, which guarantees even more trouble, if not immediately, then down the road.

A further irony of all this is that a large majority of professional economists, including those aligned on the political "left" as well as "right," respond to surveys by indicating that they generally oppose "government price controls." The problem is that most government price manipulations and controls are not advertised as such. They may be stealthy by design, or they may just take a form that is not easily recognized for what it is. Whatever form they take, they are doing untold damage to the hopes and prospects of anyone who depends on the economy, especially the poor.

Chapter Three

What Prices Do for Us

I MAGINE GETTING UP one morning and discovering that there are no longer any prices. What complete chaos there would be, chaos that would soon lead to shortages, starvation, and social collapse! Without any prices, we would be back to a barter system, and the world's present population could not even be fed, housed, or clothed by barter. Prices help us survive and thrive by enormously simplifying economic life. They do not tell us everything, but they tell us enough to make decisions.

Let's say that I am a tomato sauce producer. If the price of tomato sauce is higher than the price of the inputs (tomatoes, olive oil, spices, glass jars, labels, processing facilities, etc.), I will probably decide to make tomato sauce.

I do not know why these prices are what they are. Is it because demand is rising or falling? Or is it supply? I do not need to know in order to produce (or to consume). Prices lead me and other market participants to act in ways that balance demand and supply and, by doing so, to give people as much as possible of what they want.

What happens if the flow of information from prices is interrupted by government price manipulations or controls? If I am unaware of what is happening, I may make poor decisions. If I become aware of what is happening, I may become afraid to make any decisions at all. Either way, my employees may lose their jobs or at least their raises.

During the eighteenth century, there were frequent bread shortages in France. This is when Queen Marie Antoinette is supposed to have exclaimed, when told that the peasants were starving from lack of bread, "Why, let them eat cake!" The French government was not much more sensible in dealing with the crisis. It placed price controls on bread, since scarcity was driving the price higher.

The intention was to make bread more affordable. The cost of growing wheat was also rising, however, so that the wheat farmers realized they would have to sell at a loss. Not surprisingly, they stopped planting, and the price of bread rose even higher.

Jacques Turgot, Controller-General of France, tried to introduce free price reforms. But government officials and allied business interests—crony capitalists, in today's terminology—quickly forced his resignation. This in turn sealed the fate of the regime, and eventually cost the monarch his life as well as that of his wife Marie Antoinette. In 1770, Turgot wrote that

> [The French monarchy] fanc[ied] that it ensured abundance of grain by making the condition of the cultivator more uncertain and unhappy than that of all other citizens.[5]

Governments have imposed outright price controls on goods for thousands of years. King Hammurabi literally carved prices in stone on a monument placed in ancient Babylon about four thousand years ago. As demand and supply shifted, one can only imagine the havoc caused by these legally mandated, never-changing prices.

The communist government that followed the Russian Revolution of 1917 faced a particularly troublesome decision about prices. Its leaders knew that they intended to abolish private property and private profits. In that case, what to do about prices? Should they be kept? It seemed unimaginable to abolish prices completely. But with private property and private property transactions outlawed, who would set prices and how would it be done?

This was complicated by a curious omission on Karl Marx's part. The founder of communism had never, in all three fat volumes of his work *Capital*, bothered to explain exactly how his version of socialism would work. There was no blueprint on which to draw nor even specific instructions about prices or profits.

Faced with this quandary, the Soviet planners decided that public officials would set prices and any profits would accrue to the state. British economist John Maynard Keynes praised these efforts:

> Let us not belittle these magnificent experiments or refuse to learn from them.... The Five Year Plan in Russia, the Corporative state [devised by Mussolini] in Italy;... and state planning [under] democracy in Great Britain.... Let us hope that they will all be successful.[6]

Economist Ludwig von Mises sharply disagreed with this. He argued in a 1920 article ("Economic Calculation in the Socialist Commonwealth") and a 1922 book (*Socialism*) that the Soviet system was unworkable. Prices set by government officials could not possibly provide the information needed to make efficient decisions about the allocation of capital and labor.

A flourishing modern economy requires billions of such decisions. How could government officials, however expert, know enough or learn enough to make sense of all the masses of price interrelationships or even be able to define them? Journalist John Gunther, author of *Inside USA* in 1946, wrote that:

> It goes without saying . . . that some degree
> of government intervention and control in
> economic life has become a necessity . . . be-
> cause of the enormously increased complex-
> ity . . . of the modern world. . . . [7]

But Gunther got it backward. The more complex an economy becomes, the more hopeless it is for government officials to try to control it by fiat. The Soviet planners, including some brilliant minds, tried every imaginable stratagem to make it work without a system of free market prices within a framework of competition. Over time, they developed many systems of equations that may have helped a little, but no system of equations could cope with the multidimensionality of an economy, something that private prices, directed by no one, manage with ease.

As von Mises said:

> It is not enough to tell a man not to buy on
> the cheapest market and not to sell on the
> dearest market. . . . One must establish un-
> ambiguous rules for the guidance of con-
> duct in each concrete situation. [8]

Von Mises student Friedrich Hayek added that markets are a

discovery system.

They discover what is scarce, what is available. They communicate it through prices.

Communist and many other economists tried to prove von Mises and Hayek wrong, but never got very far. By 1960, the Soviet Union, having abandoned many failed price systems, still had five to nine in operation simultaneously, according to different accounts, and probably did not actually know how many it had. None of them worked, despite the expedient of "borrowing" prices from market economies in Europe and elsewhere.[9] This failure led directly to the fall of communism.

The fall of communism is not a reason for governments of so-called market economies to congratulate themselves. They may not attempt to control all prices, as the Soviet planners did. But they are not allowing prices to tell the economic truth either.

Chapter Four

The Role of Profits in Driving Down Prices

PROFITS ARE AN integral part of any free price system. If people are free to set the prices for what they are selling, they will naturally try to set the price high enough to earn a profit. This actually works to everyone's, not just the seller's, advantage.

Some people believe that a profit margin (what the producer earns over and above cost) makes goods or services more expensive. Philosopher Ted Honderich expresses this viewpoint:

> If there are two ways of [producing] some
> valuable thing, and the second way involves
> not only the costs of [producing] it ... but

> also [unnecessary] profits of millions or
> billions of dollars or pounds, then . . . the
> second way is patently and tremendously
> less efficient.[10]

Honderich could not be more wrong. Imagine that my tomato sauce business (earlier in this chapter) is earning a very fat profit. Most likely I will take those profits and use them to increase production. I will want to increase production in order to earn even more fat profits. Other tomato sauce producers will likely do the same, and some companies not presently making tomato sauce may also be lured into the business by the high profit margin. As a direct result, the supply of tomato sauce will most likely rise, the price will fall because of the expanded supply, and profit margins will then shrink. If profit margins shrink too much, supply may fall too far, and prices rise again. Throughout this trial and error process, consumers are signaling how much tomato sauce of what kind they want. Prices and profits relay their decisions.

The chief point to take away from all this is that the quest for profits in a competitive market increases supply. Increased supply in turn lowers, not raises prices. If profit is eliminated, prices will tend to rise, not fall. This is exactly what happened in France when government restricted the price of bread in order to make it more affordable. The result was that bread became much more expensive if it could be found at all.

The quest for profits also drives businesses to try to lower their costs—the prices they pay. The best way to lower business costs is to invest profits in equipment, facilities, or worker training. Businesses that fail to invest in order to lower their costs will soon find themselves losing out to competitors.

If a business succeeds in reducing its costs, this may increase profits, but usually not for long. Studies consistently show that over time the money saved by becoming more productive is used to increase worker pay or reduce consumer prices. Why? Because businesses have to compete for workers and customers and will lose them if they do not keep wages going up and consumer prices going down.

It is not necessary for workers even to be in short supply for this effect to be felt. No business can succeed if a competitor attracts away the best workers, and even one competitor is enough to take away customers with lower prices. Since workers are also consumers, rising wages with falling consumer prices is a formula for helping the average person.

If profits are not just temporarily high in an industry, but seem to be stuck for a long time at a high plateau, and no one seems to be manipulating or controlling prices by creating a monopoly with the backing of powerful government officials, it tells us that there is some economic problem to be overcome, some bottleneck interfering with commerce. High profits then signal opportunity for the entrepreneur who can overcome the bottleneck.

For example, wheat was historically very difficult to get from farmer to market without spoiling or being eaten by rats, which enabled the hauler to charge high prices and earn a large profit. This eventually led entrepreneurs to invest in rat proof containers and also in better transportation. The price of fish also fell dramatically as entrepreneurs invested in better ships and then refrigerated ships, thereby cutting out many middle merchants and seaports. From a free price system perspective, the temporarily high profit margins did their work. They attracted ingenuity and capital and the combination helped solve an economic problem.

Even Karl Marx, of all people, agreed that the profit system reduces prices, although he still wished to abolish it. He stated in the *Communist Manifesto* of 1848:

> The cheap prices of its commodities are the heavy artillery with which [the profit system] compels all nations, on pain of extinction, to adopt the [profit] mode of production.[11]

Chapter Five

Who Are the Bosses in a Free Price System?

MARX WAS RIGHT that profits drive down prices. But don't average people, and especially the poor, benefit from these lower prices? Why then did Marx say that the profit system is run by the rich for the benefit of the rich? Wasn't he being inconsistent, or at least confusing? If it is inconsistent or confusing to hold that profits drive down prices but nevertheless help the rich instead of the poor, why did history professor and contemporary Marxist Howard Zinn deepen the mystery further by arguing that

> the profit motive . . . has . . . distorted our whole economic and social system by making profit the key to what is produced.[12]

Economist Ludwig von Mises explains why Marx and Zinn are incorrect, why the free price (and profit) system especially benefits and, without government intervention to create and protect monopoly, is ultimately controlled by the many, not the few:

> Mass production [is] the fundamental principle of [profit-seeking] industry.... Big business, the target of the most fanatic attacks by the so-called leftists, produces ... for the masses.[13]

Economist Milton Friedman develops this idea further:

> Progress ... over the past century ... has freed the masses from backbreaking toil and has made available to them products and services that were formerly the monopoly of the upper classes....[14] The rich in Ancient Greece would have ... welcomed the improvements in transportation and in medicine, but for the rest, the great achievements of [profit seeking] have redounded primarily to the benefit of the ordinary person.[15]

Henry Hazlitt is even more specific:

> The overwhelming majority of Americans ... now enjoy the advantages of running water, central heating, telephones, automobiles,

refrigerators, washing machines, [electronic
music], radios, television sets—amenities
that millionaires and kings did not enjoy
a few generations ago.[16]

We must of course now add air conditioning and
computers, which in some form are owned by a majority of poor people in America.

What about today's luxury goods? They represent
a much smaller part of the economy than production
for the masses, but cannot be said to benefit the masses.
Or do they? Many of today's luxury goods will become
tomorrow's necessities for everyone.

When luxuries first appear, they are almost always
expensive; only people with considerable means can
afford them. But as production grows, costs fall, so that
more and more people, and eventually most people can
afford them. This is how telephones, electricity, automobiles, and computers got their start as consumer
items. If there had been no luxury buyers, such products
would never have gotten a start, and no one would have
them now.

Von Mises offers an additional point. Average consumers not only benefit from a free price (and profit)
system. They also largely control it:

Descriptive terms which people use are often
quite misleading. In talking about modern cap-
tains of industry and leaders of big business, for

> instance, they call a man a "chocolate king" or
> a "cotton king" or an "automobile king." Their
> use of such terminology implies that they see
> practically no difference between the mod-
> ern heads of industry and those feudal kings,
> dukes or lords of earlier days. But the differ-
> ence is in fact very great, for a chocolate king
> does not rule at all, he serves. This "king" must
> stay in the good graces of his subjects, the con-
> sumers; he loses his "kingdom" as soon as he
> is no longer in a position to give his custom-
> ers better service and provide it at lower cost
> than others with whom he must compete.[17]

Yes, kings of old might incite a rebellion through weak or poor rule and might also face invasion from abroad, but the economic "king" is in a much more precarious position. Every day his "subjects" vote with their purchases and therefore every day he must earn their "vote" anew. In this environment, it is possible, although very rare, to become rich in a short time, but it is easy to lose one's fortune in a short time, especially if one has loans that cannot be repaid.

The concept of consumer economic control was artic-ulated in 1928 by British economist Edwin Cannan. He wrote that

> [some] try to convince the wage-earners
> that they are working not for the public and

not for the consumers of the things or services which they produce, but for the capitalist employer, [but this is just political] propaganda.[18]

Beatrice Potter, a founder with her husband Sidney Webb of Fabian Socialism, disputed Cannan:

In the business of my father everybody had to obey the orders issued by my father, the boss. He alone had to give orders, but to him nobody gave any orders.[19]

Ludwig von Mises in turn corrected Potter:

This is a very short-sighted view. Orders were given to her father by the consumers, by the buyers. Unfortunately [Potter] could not see these orders.[20]

As we shall see in subsequent chapters, producers often try to escape the sovereignty of the consumer and the accompanying discipline of market competition. They do this by creating monopolies and by other means, but they usually require the assistance of government to succeed for very long. When this happens, it is no longer a free price system, but a crony capitalist system.

Chapter Six

"Spontaneous Order" from Free Prices

I N A GENUINE free price system, which governments historically have never allowed, consumers as a whole would lead the economy. No one person or elite would have much say about the direction we take. Some people find this idea disturbing. Would it not lead to chaos? Can any system thrive which is unguided, rudderless, subject to no visible commands? Would this not lead to trouble? The answer is quite simple: no.

A system led by consumers will produce by far the best outcome for consumers. Whom should an economy serve if not consumers? As we have noted, all workers are consumers, although not all consumers are workers.

Our economic system should not revolve around the supposed needs of workers and certainly not around the supposed needs of business owners, but rather around the needs of consumers and then everyone, workers and business owners included, will benefit.

A system led by consumers is an example of what Michael Polanyi called a

spontaneous order.[21]

Some of our most important and reliable human systems work this way. Everything works admirably with no commands from any government guiding authority. In the case of religion, the US constitution forbids government direction or control. This was a major departure from historical precedent, since previously government and religion had almost always been combined in some way in human societies. And most people would agree it was a necessary and fruitful reform.

But there is much more in our society that is not directed in any way by government. For example, who directs human language? The French Academy has attempted to direct how people speak French, but no one pays much attention. Our common law has accumulated over the centuries in a similar way, unguided by any central government authority. If we do not need government controlling our religion, our language, or the evolution of our common law, why do we need government controlling our economic price system?

Social philosopher Walter Lippmann wrote of the

> uncoordinated, unplanned, disorderly individualism[22]

of a free market economy, but he was wrong about it being unplanned. As economist Friedrich Hayek explained:

> This is not a dispute about whether planning is to be done or not. It is a dispute as to whether planning is to be done centrally, by one authority for the whole economic system, or is to be divided among many individuals.[23]

Dividing economic leadership among billions of people creates a much more reliable and ordered system than any form of central control. It is also the only possible safeguard against monopoly, because in a centralized, government-controlled system, economic predators need only make a deal with the government to create an unassailable monopoly.

It is often argued that the defect of a free price system is that it will over time fall into the hands of a few predatory business concerns. But when we look closely at economic history, this is almost impossible to do without government collusion. It is government that holds the power to fine, jail, or kill. It is government which can bankrupt through prolonged legal proceedings. Without these powers protecting them, would-be monopolists have little chance of destroying all competition.

Putting the economy into billions of hands rather than into the hands of a few government leaders is also a safer approach. There is no way to avoid economic mistakes, but if decisions are made by individual producers and consumers, they will be made on a small scale, and therefore easily corrected, unlike the often catastrophic mistakes of central planners.

The failure of the Communist planners is a warning. So is President Franklin Roosevelt's failure to end the Great Depression. So is the Crash of 2008, primarily caused by US Federal Reserve and other central bank errors, which we will explore further in this book. Adam Smith explained this basic point in 1776:

> The statesman, who would attempt to direct private people in what manner they ought to employ their capitals, would not only load himself with a most unnecessary attention, but assume an authority which could safely be trusted, not only to no single person, but to no council or senate whatever, and which would nowhere be so dangerous as in the hands of a man who had folly and presumption enough to fancy himself fit to exercise it.[24]

Chapter Seven

The Essential Role of Loss and Bankruptcy

THE ENTIRE PRICE and profit system is objectively scored. If you make investments, you either make a profit or you suffer a loss. There is no ambiguity about it, provided that accounting is honest. If you suffer large enough losses, and especially if you have debts to repay, you may go bankrupt. This is extremely important. As economist Wilhelm Röpke has explained:

> Since the fear of loss appears to be of more moment than the desire for gain, it may be said that our economic system (in the final analysis) is regulated by bankruptcy.[25]

It is the special genius of the profit system that it persuades people to change or at least to accept change in order to win a profit or to avoid a loss. Human beings are often reluctant to accept change, even when change is necessary or desirable. Governments and their bureaucracies are, as a general rule, notoriously unwilling to change.

Why does the United States still maintain 54,000 troops in Germany in 2012, at very great expense, so many years after the end of World War II and the Cold War with the Soviet Union? Germany spends barely more than one percent of its gross domestic product on defense, much less than the United States. Why is the once-thriving city of Detroit bankrupt, with so many of its buildings boarded up or completely abandoned? Why do government leaders promise to balance their budgets, but fail to reach agreement on how to do it and just keep falling deeper and deeper in debt, to the point that the debt can never realistically be repaid at all? The reason is that governments, even democratic governments, do not have any built-in mechanism to force needed change, as the profit system forces failing businesses to change.

Governments are also reinforced in their resistance to change by entrenched economic interests that benefit from the status quo. It is the industries of today, not the emerging industries of the future, that have money to spend on elections and thus access to government leaders. These entrenched interests use all their influence with government to try to outlaw or at least slow down upstart competitors offering better ways of doing things. When they get into really deep trouble, they demand and receive public bailouts.

Passing laws to restrict such crony behavior is difficult enough; enforcing them is impossible. Nor is it a panacea to break up the largest companies. There are economies of scale to be gained from large-scale production, so that an artificial limit on company size will just result in economic inefficiency and needlessly higher prices. These matters are best left to consumers to sort out through a truly free price system operating within a framework of competition.

Karl Marx recognized that the free price system pushes people to create or at least accept change. He did not like this and characterized it as

> uninterrupted disturbance of all social conditions, everlasting uncertainty and agitation. . . . All fixed, fast-frozen relations are swept away. . . . All that is solid melts into air.[26]

Well, perhaps, but economic growth assumes change. Without change, the human race would still be hunting and gathering. Very few of us would have been born or would have survived in such a precarious environment. Even so, at any given moment, the forces opposing change in a society are usually stronger than the forces favoring it.

Outside of a free price and profit system, the only way to achieve change is through government coercion. This is unlikely because, as noted, governments usually oppose change. Even in the few instances where a revolutionary government demands change, whether for good or ill, it is not usually able to bend people to its will for very long. Human beings devise passive-aggressive strategies to resist orders from above. Sheer terror, as practiced by Stalin, can overcome this kind of resistance for a time. But even the most brutal methods will ultimately falter, and how can an economy possibly innovate, grow, and thrive in a climate of fear and murder?

Russia and China recognized this when they finally abandoned the Stalinist and Maoist systems of terror, but each has still clung to residual methods of government control and coercion. It is not surprising that, as a result, Russian economic growth has been poor. Chinese economic growth is hard to gauge because of phony government statistics and also marred by tremendous environmental devastation. But as in Russia the economy is beset by tremendous corruption, all of which continually threatens the economic gains that have been made through the reduction in terror.

The most effective human regulation is self-regulation, regulation that people voluntarily choose for themselves. The free price system is the prime example of a self-regulatory system and the greatest success story in human history. Through a combination of carrots and sticks, it leads people to want to make the changes that ultimately improve our standard of living.

Price manipulations and controls by government are often described as regulations. But to the degree that they undermine the natural regulation of the free price system, they actually destabilize our economic and social system. Human societies' economies require the additional regulation of a legal system. Everyone needs to understand and abide by the rules of the game. But insofar as so-called government regulation undermines market regulation, it is dysregulating.

Chapter Eight

What About Inequality?

T HE FREE PRICE SYSTEM indisputably produces unequal economic outcomes. About this, the economist John Maynard Keynes said that

> I want to mold a society in which most of the [economic] inequalities and causes of inequality are removed.[27]

Most people tend to agree with this—until they think through what it would mean to try to achieve it

Consider, for example, the French Revolutionary slogan "liberty, equality, fraternity." On close inspection, there is something completely illogical about this. The ideals of liberty and equality are incompatible. If people are free, they will behave differently, which will lead to different outcomes. If I save and my friend does not, in the long run I should end up with a higher income, perhaps much higher. Should this be forbidden? And if so, how to forbid it? If government deprives us of liberty, ostensibly to enforce equality, as was done in the Soviet Union, the enforcers will themselves become a higher class with special privileges.

The enforcement of an ideology of equality has produced some of the most barbarous episodes in world history. Consider the story of a group of idealistic Americans from the Upper Midwest who in the 1930s decided that they did not want to live in a society propelled by "greed," but would instead volunteer their services in the "worker's paradise" of the Soviet Union. This led them to save, hire a boat, and embark for Russia.

On arrival, the volunteers were met by Soviet officials and were marched, perhaps singing Socialist songs, toward a work camp. There they were brutally enslaved and put to hard labor with little food and insufficient clothing or shelter to withstand the cold. Few are believed to have survived. Better-known incidents include the massacre in Cambodia by Pol Pot of everyone with a degree of education, the extermination of the Kulaks by Stalin, and the Great Leap Forward and Cultural Revolution of Mao in China—in all of which many millions died.

To recognize that liberty and equality are logical opposites, or to cite such episodes, does not, however, make a complete argument against the desire to find a balance where freedom is subject to rules and where we can achieve a more equal society.

None of us want to see other people in need. Most of us think that we should try to help those who, for whatever reason, are suffering or living in abject poverty. The real problem is not lack of complete equality, but rather that some people simply do not have enough. The inescapable question is how best to go about addressing this problem. Is it to earn money and give a portion to charity, in addition to helping others get a start in the market system by educating, training, and hiring them? Or is it to restrict free prices and profits, or even to abolish the free price and profit system altogether?

To answer this, we will have to ask what works best. But we will also need to consider morality. American Socialist Michael Harrington has stated that

[the profit system] is outrageously unjust.

Is this right? Are incomes determined by the free price and profit system both

arbitrary

and

inequitable,

as John Maynard Keynes asserted?[28]

It is hard to see how our incomes are in any sense arbitrary. They are determined, like everything else in the free price system, by demand and supply. Norman Van Cott has explained that

> our incomes—be they large, small or somewhere in between—reflect (1) our usefulness to our fellow citizens and (2) the ease with which fellow citizens can find substitutes for us.[29]

It is natural to object that people are not commodities. But our labor is not our self. Our labor (unlike our self) is a commodity and can be priced like any other commodity. This is not unjust. It is reality.

Most government policies designed to alleviate the reality of labor as commodity just backfire. A minimum wage means that young people are never hired and are therefore never trained. A minimum government guaranteed income (or its equivalent in free services such as housing, food, and medicine) means that some people may not choose to be hired, which eventually will bankrupt the system. The idea that government can train workers is fanciful. Only real work can train workers. Even the best education is not real training although it is useful if it instills basic knowledge and good personal work habits.

It is also true that there is a large element of luck in this. Some of us are indeed lucky to be born with brains, to attend good schools, or even to inherit money. All of these things make it easier to get more money. But getting money is not the only, or even the most important, way that we are lucky or unlucky. As economist Robert Sowell has noted:

> The difference between a factory worker and an executive is nothing compared to the difference between being born brain-damaged and being born normal, or the difference between being born to loving parents rather than abusive parents.[30]

The principle of equality of opportunity does not mean that everyone has the same opportunity. Life will not permit that. It means that society should not deliberately discriminate against anyone, and it is consistent with a free price system. Indeed a free price system logically demands it. A business owner in a free price system who refuses to serve customers or hire people based on some personal prejudice will just lose access to customers or the best employees and thereby lose ground against the competition.

But if we are going to try to level all the playing fields and create equality of outcome, where do we start? And how can we do it without robbing people of their right to live life as they see fit? For example, do you want everyone to have the same medical care? What if you personally think that the medical care in question is harmful rather than helpful? There is always a great deal of disagreement in medicine, which is the only reason there is medical progress.

Will we insist on the same drug for the same malady? But is it the same malady, given our biological differences? Research suggests that most drugs are only effective for a minority of those who take them, because we are all very different biologically. The same drug and dose for infant, young, middle-aged, and old? If not, who will choose the drug or define the age brackets? And on what basis? In the end, any such efforts defy common sense and logic as well as our right to make our own choices about ourselves, so long as we do not aggress against or harm others.

Even if this is acknowledged, some will want to restrict free prices in an effort to reduce inequality, if only a bit. Economist Arthur Okun, a chairman of the President's Council of Economic Advisors during the 1960s, personally favored

complete [economic] equality,[31]

but thought that sacrificing some economic efficiency and growth for greater "equity" would be a reasonable compromise.

The trouble with this idea is that personal incomes are prices. When government tries to manipulate or control these prices, the result is not likely to be income redistribution. It is more likely to be wealth destruction.

Wealth is not something we pick up on the beach and share among ourselves. It has to be created through hard work, investment, insight, and oversight. Schemes of redistribution just reduce or destroy it for everyone, with particularly unfortunate consequences for the poor.

Wealth may be rapidly destroyed when taxed. Estate taxes take chosen investments carefully chosen over a lifetime, often by the most experienced and successful investors, and liquidate them so that government can spend more. This is not a good trade-off for the economy because private investment is the engine of job creation. Even larger-scale wealth taxation would mean so many shares and properties dumped onto markets to be converted into cash that market values of all assets would collapse. The only alternative would be for the government to become the owner of the assets. The Communists tried that and it did not succeed.

Another important point to keep in mind about inequality has been noted by economist Milton Friedman:

> Nowhere is the gap between rich and poor wider, nowhere are the rich richer and the poor poorer, than in those countries that do not permit the free market to operate.[32]

There is extensive evidence to support Friedman's assertion, including a notable World Bank study from economists David Dollar and Aart Kraay.[33]

Chapter Nine

Why Greed Is Not "Good" in a Free Price System

WE HAVE ALREADY seen that the price system encourages us to value, or at least accept, change, but it teaches us much more besides. It also teaches us to work hard, to defer gratification, to save rather than spend on ourselves. As a corollary of this, it encourages us to be patient, to keep our eyes fixed on the long term, which means decades at least, not just the short term.

For example, if I start a business with $50,000 in initial sales and grow this at a fairly rapid 15% a year, it will take eighteen years to reach $400,000. In another eighteen years, sales will reach $3.2 million; in another eighteen years, $25.6 million. If I survive for another eighteen years, I will see $205 million. As these numbers suggest, for a long time, the business will seem to be progressing at a snail's pace. But if the growth rate can be maintained, the compounding of even larger numbers will produce stupendous returns. One more eighteen years to compound, and the business will have grown to $1.6 billion in annual sales.

The founders of McDonald's and of Coca-Cola sold out in the first few years, and thus missed a chance to become enormously rich. The lesson is clear: have faith, stick with it, and do not let the first money you earn go to your head.

What else does the price system teach us? Critics say that it teaches us to be selfish and greedy. Is that true? The philosopher and novelist Ayn Rand, a famous defender of "free markets," would have answered: certainly, and a good thing at that.

Rand assumed that everyone is greedy, and that free markets directed aggression into constructive channels. This is not a new idea. Samuel Johnson, eighteenth-century wise man and wit, suggested that

> there are few ways in which a man can be more innocently employed than in getting money.[34]

Economist John Maynard Keynes quipped

> it is better that a man tyrannize over his bank balance than over his fellow-citizens.[35]

Keynes was not a proponent of the "greed is good" school, but did state that

> avarice and usury must be our gods for a little longer still. For only they can lead us out of the tunnel of economic necessity into daylight.[36]

Eighteenth-century economist Adam Smith offered a memorable defense—not of greed, but of rational self-interest, which does not seek to take from others what is rightfully theirs—when he declared that

> it is not from the benevolence of the butcher, the brewer, or the baker, that we expect our dinner, but from their regard to their own interest. We address ourselves, not to their humanity but to their self-love, and never talk to them of our own necessities but of their advantages.[37]

> . . . He generally, indeed, neither intends to promote the public interest, nor knows how much he is promoting it. . . . He intends only his own gain, and he is in this, as in many other cases, led by an invisible hand to promote an end which was no part of his intention.[38]

The motivational speaker Zig Ziglar turned this into some useful personal advice:

> You can have everything in life you want,
> if you'll just help enough other people get
> what they want.[39]

Adam Smith went on to argue that

> whenever commerce is introduced into any
> country, probity[,] punctuality[,] ... econ-
> omy, industry, [and] discretion ... always
> accompany it. These virtues in a rude and
> barbarous country are almost unknown.[40, 41]

But, according to Smith, it is rational self-interest that promotes these personal and civic virtues.

Could Rand, Keynes, and even Smith be mistaken about the values taught by the free price system? Yes. This system is not teaching us to be greedy, or even directing that greed into more constructive channels. Nor is it only promoting rational self-interest. It is instead teaching us to stop thinking about our own needs and wishes and start focusing on the needs and wishes of others, in particular our employees and customers. If we try to do this only from rational self-interest, we will not find it easy. If we care genuinely about others and about our contribution to society, it will be much easier to stay the course, which typically is very long and demanding.

A brash, young entrepreneur may think he is entering business to become rich or famous or enjoy life. But he will soon learn that the rewards are distant and uncertain while the personal sacrifices are immediate. Most people do not like to work seven days a week, watch every penny of personal expense, or give up control over their own time.

We have already seen that a "boss" of a successful business is not just a "boss," but also a willing servant of others. Someone may "fake" this attitude for a while, but will ultimately be found out. Predation, exploitation, parasitism—all of these may augment the profits of a single transaction or a single year. But the worth of a business is defined as the "present value" of all future profits, and in a free price system, free of government-created and -protected monopolies, predatory practices do not amplify but rather destroy future profits.

If a business owner must put the needs of employees and customers first, what about competitors? Is not market competition a cutthroat, dog-eat-dog business, with predation the rule rather than the exception? Once again, this is a false picture.

Most competition takes place within an organized, cooperative framework, similar to the Olympics. Olympic athletes can be as competitive as they like, but must conform to the rules of fair competition, which also include no collusion, or they will lose their medals, as some have done.

In some cases, business competition is much more collegial than sports. Wheat farmers, for example, technically compete with one another, but think of themselves as colleagues, not competitors. Competitors in other industries may behave very differently. In any case, there is only one durable way to out-compete other firms, and that is to serve your employees, and through them, your customers, better and better. This is the only true competitive advantage—anything else is ephemeral.

Young people sometimes eschew business and enter government or the non-profit sector because they want to make the world a better place. But if they consider, they will realize that businesses exist to meet the tangible needs of people, just as government and non-profits do. And of course some people enter public service for anything but altruistic reasons: they may be attracted by the lure of fame or power rather than money.

Values inculcated by the free price system are demanding. They often take generations to learn. Once learned, they make the world not only a more productive place, but a better place in which to live.

It is not surprising that proponents of the free price system led the battle against world slavery in the eighteenth and nineteenth centuries. And they were not only opposed to slavery. They were also opposed to nationalism, tribalism, racism, and sectarianism as well.

The free price system teaches us to tolerate, work with, and ultimately appreciate people of all lands and conditions. If we do not, we will lose our best employees and many potential customers. As noted before, this is not just a matter of calculation. Either we believe it or we do not. In the long run, people will not be fooled.

Economist George Stigler understands all this:

> Important as the moral influences of the marketplace are, they have not been subjected to any real study. The immense proliferation of general education, of scientific progress, and of democracy are all coincidental in time and place with the emergence of the free enterprise system of organizing the marketplace. I believe this coincidence was not accidental.[42]

Economist Geoffrey Martin Hodgson does not understand free price system values:

> The firm has to compete not simply for profit but for our confidence and trust. To achieve this, it has to abandon profit-maximization, or even shareholder satisfaction, as the exclusive objectives of the organization.[43]

This is hopelessly wrong. The only way we can maximize profits is to earn the confidence and trust of our customers. These two activities are not mutually exclusive. They are one and the same.

Economist John Kenneth Galbraith, past president of the American Economic Association, and best-selling author, also demonstrates a complete lack of understanding when he writes that there is nothing reliable to be learned about making money. If there were, study would be intense and everyone with a positive IQ would be rich.[44]

But it is not a high IQ, or a business degree, that enables us to make money. It is a strong desire to serve others, not just ourselves, along with sound judgment about how to go about it, since, in business as in life, good intentions are not enough.

Lesson Three

Enemies of the
Free Price System

Chapter Ten

Crony Capitalism

THE STRUGGLE TO establish free and honest prices in competitive markets is thousands of years old. For most of that time, powerful private interests, allied with even more powerful government officials, protected the opposite system of manipulated or controlled prices that has persisted through every era and always dominated the economic system.

For most of history, this state of affairs never really had a name. It was just the "system" and everyone accepted it as the norm. Human beings were organized into tribes. Tribes had rulers, wealthy people allied themselves with the rulers, and below them the common people subsisted on what the powerful and rich did not take for themselves.

During the eighteenth century, when critics finally emerged in numbers, it began to be called mercantilism. In the twentieth century, it had many names, but in this book will be called crony capitalism.* The advantage of this terminology is that it makes a clear distinction between this system and the concept of capitalism. Whatever the merit or demerit of the concept of capitalism (which in turn depends on how the term is defined), it is not the same as crony capitalism. The latter may for publicity purposes pretend to support a free price system, but this is just camouflage for its utter and usually ruthless rejection of a free price system.

The very earliest historical record of what might now be called crony capitalism dates to ancient China. Han Dynasty annals tell us that the Emperor Wu-di (155–87 BCE) decided that government must control the economy, and castrated his advisor Sima Qian for daring to dispute his view. Although Wu-di said that he was setting up monopolies granted by the state in salt, iron, and other basic commodities in order to protect the common people from greedy merchants, his monopolies really just made a few merchants colossally rich, and ensured a steady stream of kickbacks from them to court officials and to the Emperor himself.

---

* William Safire reported in 1998 that he had traced the first appearance of this phrase to a 1981 *Time Magazine* article written by unidentified staff.

Almost two thousand years later, the Scottish economist Adam Smith restated Sima's case in words strikingly reminiscent of the early Chinese master's own:

> The natural effort of every individual to better his own condition, when suffered to exert itself with freedom and security, is not only capable of carrying on the society to wealth and prosperity, but of surmounting an hundred impertinent obstructions with which the folly of human laws too often encumbers its operations.[45]

In the meantime, the middle and later Roman emperors imitated Wu-di. They granted monopolies, instituted price controls punishable by death, debased the currency by stripping precious metals from coins, exacted ever harsher taxation, and reaped a whirlwind of corruption and economic collapse As economist Jesus Huerta de Soto has written:

> Roman civilization did not fall as a result of the barbarian invasions. It undermined itself from within through its own economic policies, although serious plagues also played a part in decimating and demoralizing the population.[46]

In Sung China (tenth century, CE), merchants were classed with undertakers and other "unclean" groups,[47] and the government did not hesitate to confiscate mercantile fortunes that came to its attention, a pattern that persisted throughout Chinese imperial history. The great historian of commerce and capitalism, Fernand Braudel, acknowledges that

> In the vast world of Islam, especially prior to the eighteenth century, ownership was temporary, for there, as in China, [property] legally belonged to the prince. When the [rich person] died, his seigneury and all his possessions reverted to the Sultan of Istanbul or the Great Mogul of Delhi.[48] [In addition,] André Raymond's recent study of eighteenth century Cairo shows us that the great merchants there rarely were able to maintain their positions for more than a generation. They were devoured by political society.[49]

The historian David Landes records the same thing in Japan. He cites the case of Yodoya Tatsugoro, scion of the leading commercial family in Osaka. The family had made itself immensely rich, had also performed many services to the nation, and had regularly lent money to the ruling classes. These loans could not be refused, but once made, they led to strained relations In the end, all the family's money was confiscated by the government on the grounds that Yodoya was "living beyond his social status."[50]

Landes describes an even more predatory environment in the Ottoman (Turkish) empire of the fourteenth–early twentieth centuries:

> The Ottomans had ... taken over a region once strong, now enfeebled—looting as they went. Now they could no longer take from outside. They had to generate wealth from within, to promote productive investment. Instead, they resorted to habit and tried to pillage the interior, to squeeze their own subjects. Nothing, not even the wealth of high officials, was secure. Nothing could be more self-destructive.[51]

Looking back over world history, and especially more modern history, governments have gradually become wiser than the Ottoman Sultans. They have learned that it is better to let private capital accumulate, to pluck the goose of private enterprise, not to kill it. But even so they are tempted to make "minor deals" that turn out to be anything but minor in their consequences. For example, in seventeenth-century France, the rich woolen, silk, and linen producers persuaded the government to ban the import or production of cotton cloth, which was then a new product, in order to protect themselves from competition. On one level, this produced rather comical results as government spies began

> peering into coaches and private houses and reporting that the governess of the Marquis

de Cormoy had been seen at her window
clothed in calico of a white background
with big red flowers, almost new.[52]

All was not gossip and amusement, however. Enforcement of the rules led many thousands of ordinary people to be executed or sent into gruesome labor on ships. Perhaps most importantly, Britain created its industrial revolution and surged ahead economically by producing cotton textiles, while France's refusal to allow cotton meant that it stagnated and fell far behind.

Chapter Eleven

Laissez-Faire
Contra the Cronies

I N REVIEWING A very few ronytories from the long history of crony capitalism, we confront a paradox. Government exists to protect us from private violence, theft, and fraud. But, once it is established, who will guard us from the guardians? We can walk away forever from a bad boss, merchant, or customer, but we cannot walk away from the government.

Given the extreme difficulty of establishing effective and honest government, it is not surprising that most human beings have remained in desperate poverty during the thousands of years of recorded, so-called civilized life. Until the eighteenth century, the human economy as a whole barely grew at all, and even since then the rate of growth has not been exceptional. Why is this? Economist John Maynard Keynes wrote that

> The destruction of the inducement to invest by [a tendency to keep what wealth one had under a mattress] was the outstanding evil, the prime impediment to the growth of wealth, in the ancient and medieval worlds.[53]

But Keynes neglected to mention that people hid their money because they feared theft, and they especially feared theft by government. He was even more fanciful or perhaps disingenuous in suggesting that twentieth-century governments would decide economic issues based on "long views, the general social advantage[,] and collective wisdom."[54] All of this seems to have been premised on government officials doing what he told them to do. At other times, Keynes described government officials as "boobies."[55]

The most-often proposed remedy for this problem is to try to rein in the state and especially to restrict its role in the economy. The case for a state that acts only as an economic umpire, not an economic leader, that scrupulously limits itself to setting rules that apply to everyone, that does not try to intervene to assist any person or persons, or otherwise pursue its own economic aims and objectives—that case has been made in many eras and in many countries. Boisguilbert asked the French government in the early eighteenth century to "*laissez-*

faire la nature," by which he meant to get out of the way of commerce.[56]

Advocates of laissez-faire thought they were applying basic logic to the problem at hand: if crony capitalism represents an illicit alliance of government and private interests in the economy, the only sure way to combat it is to separate economy from state, just as the US constitution separates church from state.

This doctrine, embraced by many of the leading minds of the late eighteenth and early nineteenth centuries in Britain, America, and elsewhere, including most of the American founders, was not, as most think today, an attempt to hold down the working classes or give free rein to abusive bosses. They were not advocating sweatshop conditions for workers or child labor.

On the contrary, these reformers began by seeking to free middle-class merchants from the strangling economic cronyism of the courts. Over time, they came to embrace a multitude of beliefs that came to be known as "liberalism," and then later "classical liberalism," to differentiate them from Franklin Roosevelt's version of the term. Had these reformers not succeeded to at least a small degree in Britain and then the United States, it is very doubtful that the Industrial Revolution of these two countries would ever have happened, or would have subsequently spread to other countries.

The early laissez-faire reformers generally agreed that banning slavery, child labor, or inhuman working conditions is legitimately part of the umpire's role. British Member of Parliament Richard Cobden (1804–1865), one of the principal leaders of the movement (and over a century later cited by US President Ronald Reagan as a key influence on his thinking), insisted on getting government out of a leadership role in the economy. But he voted for restrictions on child labor as well as for more child education. Like other laissez-faire reformers, he also fought for broadening the right to vote and the removal of restrictions on women and Jews.[57]

American churches, constitutionally separated from government, and mostly governed within their own moral framework, are still subject to strict national laws. The laissez-faire idea was that the economy should operate in a similar way. In this view, there is no discipline more severe than market discipline, which is why businesses try so hard to escape it with government assistance. The discipline of market competition, which compels producers to justify everything they do in order to win and hold customers, will provide more protection for workers and especially children than laws alone, especially when the government enforcers of law can be bought.

Advocates of laissez-faire have long become accustomed to having their words distorted or fall on deaf ears in most countries and most eras. Not long before the French Revolution, Jacques Turgot was appointed Comptroller-General of France and tried in twenty brief months to reform the tottering economic system along free price, competitive market lines. But he was forced to resign, thereby sealing the fate of Louis XVI and the old regime. Étienne Bonnot, the Abbé de Condillac, exclaimed that "experience teaches [government] nothing. How many mistakes have been made! How many times have they been repeated! And they are still repeated!"[58]

Although laissez-faire reforms failed in this instance and throughout most of history, they made a little headway in Britain and America in the late eighteenth and early nineteenth century. The historian Lord Macaulay observed that, as a result, at least in Britain,

> profuse government expenditure, heavy taxation, absurd commercial restriction, corrupt tribunals, disastrous wars, persecutions, conflagrations, inundations, have not been able to destroy capital so fast as the exertions of private citizens have been able to create it.[59]

Chapter Twelve

Today's Crony Capitalism

ONE CAN ONLY imagine what the nineteenth-century laissez-faire reformers would have thought of life at the beginning of the twenty-first century in Zimbabwe, a country once described as the "breadbasket" of Africa, but which writhed in misery under the iron grip of Robert Mugabe's government. Land redistribution schemes had turned over much of the best cropland to Mugabe supporters who had not the slightest knowledge of farming. As a result, over half of the country's 12 million people were on the brink of starvation. In many cases, government opponents were forcibly relocated to remote rural areas with no means of subsistence at all.

In towns, gasoline supplies had long since disappeared, although rumors caused people periodically to race to closed pumps to see if anything had arrived. Everything was price controlled, often at a price well below the cost of production. To avoid evasion of the price controls, no "new" product, brand, or packaging could be sold without prior written permission from one of the ministries, which always of course required a bribe. The economy as a whole was estimated to be imploding at a rate of 10% a year, but property and market values had already lost 99% of their previous value.[60] Throughout all this, Mugabe gave speeches railing against "greedy entrepreneurs, ruthless markets and the forces of globalization."[61]

Nor was rampant crony capitalism limited to poor or small countries. Many of the American, European, Chinese, and Russian mega-rich of the 1990s and 2000s got their vast new wealth through government favors or connections or by understanding how government worked. This was just as true on Wall Street in the US as in Beijing or Moscow. Wall Street had first use of all the new money printed by the Federal Reserve during the "bubble years" beginning in the mid-1990s. It made as much profit in the first three years under President Obama as in the prior eight years under President George W. Bush, notwithstanding the intervening Crash that helped elect Obama on a platform of "hope and change."

Following the Crash of 2008, Sol Sanders, columnist for a "conservative" newspaper, wrote that President

Obama should "begin weekly meetings in closed session with a group of recognized private-sector leaders to brainstorm recovery strategy and tactics."[62] No worse advice can be imagined. Such a meeting—behind closed doors no less—would not be a recipe for job creation. It would be a recipe for more of the cronyism that had already destroyed millions of jobs and brought the economy to the brink of ruin in the Crash.

Whom would the president invite? Which of the powerful private economic interests that despise open, honest, competitive markets and conspire with government to prevent any change from threatening them? Would it be the then head of the president's outside economic council, the CEO of General Electric, which had just been rescued by the government and was also a major government contractor? The heads of the major banks that had been bailed out and were still being bailed out by the Federal Reserve? A firm like Goldman Sachs which, although not a bank, had been given access to the loan window at the Fed as if it were a bank, and thus could borrow billions of newly created government money at close to zero cost?

Would it be the heads of drug companies whose government-granted monopolies have been zealously guarded, with threats of jail as well as fines, by the Food and Drug Administration (FDA), an agency drug companies directly fund? The head of General Motors, also recently bailed out by government, in a way that blatantly violated bankruptcy law, that took every last penny from the mom and pop bond and warranty holders, and turned the company over to the same union that had destroyed it? Monsanto, whose controversial GMO seed, food, and insecticide/herbicide products had been virtually strong-armed into other countries by the US government, as Wikileaks documents revealed?

Such access to government leaders in a crony capitalist economy is worth a lot. How much? Here is one measure. When word of Timothy Geithner's selection to be President Obama's treasury secretary leaked, the stocks of companies considered close to him immediately jumped by an average of 15%.[63] This is hardly surprising. Geithner had already saved many of these companies billions of dollars when, as president of the New York Fed, he had quietly vetoed a plan for banks to take losses on their contracts with failed insurer AIG, and had instead decided that the government, that is the taxpayers, would absorb the loss.[64]

Eighteenth-century economist Adam Smith warned that

> People of the same trade seldom meet together, even for merriment and diversion, but the conversation ends in a conspiracy against the public, or in some contrivance to raise prices.

How much worse, then, if these merchants are meeting behind closed doors with the president of the US or secretary of the Treasury? The Obama White House presumably understands the potential value of such meetings, because it first offered to provide full logs of all White House visitors, pointedly excluding the first nine months, and then began scheduling lobbyist visits outside the White House, at the nearby Jackson Place offices, where the promise of logs was deemed not to apply, or even at coffee houses.[65]

By the end of President Obama's eight years in 2016, the *New York Times*, a fervid supporter, claimed that the administration had enjoyed an unparalleled scandal-free record. Here are just a few counterfactual examples. When the President finally got his tax increase on the rich passed at 2 A.M. on January 1, 2013 (the "fiscal cliff" bill), in the very same legislation he included massive federal giveaways to favored industries donating to him. The giveaways more than canceled any revenue gain to the treasury from the tax increases. In effect, taxes on the rich had not been increased; money had just been shifted from one group of the rich to another.

Obama's stimulus bill of 2009, supposedly about infrastructure projects such as roads and bridges, directed much of its money to friendly state and local governments to cover their expanding payrolls and deficits, as well as to friendly private interest donors. According to one study, 71% of the funds going to green energy grantees benefiting from the bill were also friendly political donors.[66]

Many of these crony system players were not even US citizens. About 70% of the money newly minted by the Fed after the 2008 Crash went to support foreign banks. An MSNBC headline read: "Wind at Their Backs: Powerful Democrats Help Chinese Energy Firm Chase Stimulus Money." The article explained how Senator Reid (D-NV) received campaign money from a Chinese project's backers.[67] Under US law, foreign nationals may legally contribute to US federal and state campaigns, so long as they hold a green card. A complaint was also filed with the Federal Election Commission of massive money coming into the Obama campaign from overseas with no real idea of its source. The FEC apparently buried the complaint.

The goal of cronyism is of course to form lucrative alliances that serve the purposes of both special interests and government officials. There is also an understanding that enmity between these powerful forces can be costly for both. The classic example was when "citizen" challenges began to be filed during the Nixon administration in the early 1970s to take away the lucrative television broadcast licenses of the *Washington Post*. Ben Bradlee, the *Post*'s editor, later described the *Post*'s reaction:

> Our stock price nosedived as the word got out that the *Post* was going to lose its TV station income. It was a scary time, and it

had an absolutely critical impact on us internally. From that time on we knew Nixon
hated us and we reciprocated. Without that,
the *Post* would never have behaved so confidently in its reporting of Watergate [which
led to Nixon's resignation].[68]

As this clearly states, a crony battle over TV licenses
was instrumental in the destruction of a presidency.

Most of the many "deals" involving the president or
Congress, like the story of the *Post*'s TV licenses in 1973,
are rarely covered by the press. Most crony capitalism
operates on a more prosaic level behind closed doors,
and receives even less coverage. For example, the US
Department of Agriculture is supposed to protect the
public from contaminated meat. But when small meat
producers proposed to test each cow slaughtered for
mad cow disease, a deadly illness transferable to humans,
the Department repeatedly ruled in the early 2000s that
such testing could not be done.

In issuing this edict, the department sided with large
meat producers who not only wished to avoid the cost
of testing, but also wanted to use the power of government to prevent smaller producers from gaining a
sales advantage from doing so. The regulators saw large
meat packers, not the general public, as their clients.[69]
To learn about this, one had to consult trade publi-
cations, because the larger media could not care less.

Smaller-scale deals take place every day in statehouses and city halls, with even less scrutiny.

A few committed believers in government control of the economy, and especially of prices, are willing to admit that their ideas have not lived up to expectations. Nevertheless, as Ludwig von Mises pointed out,

> Government interference with business is still very popular. As soon as someone does not like something that happens in the world, he says: "The government ought to do something about it. What do we have a government for?"[70]

Philosopher Michael Novak, who once believed in state leadership himself, shakes his head at this:

> One of the most astonishing characteristics of our age is that ideas, even false and unworkable ideas, even ideas which are no longer believed in by their official guardians, rule the affairs of men and run roughshod over stubborn facts. Ideas of enormous destructiveness, cruelty, and impracticality retain the allegiance of elites that benefit from them . . . .[71] [or feel that abandoning them would] violate . . . a taboo.[72]

Chapter Thirteen

The Crony Capitalist Conundrum

ECONOMIC TEXTBOOKS REFER somewhat misleadingly to "public" and "private" sectors. Before the rapid expansion of the federal government by the George W. Bush and Obama administrations, the public sector (including federal, state, and local) was thought to represent about a third of the economy. The non-profit sector, often overlooked, accounted for another 10%. This math suggested that just a bit over half of the economy was "private, for-profit." But taking into account companies that are directly or indirectly controlled by government, at least two-thirds of the economy is really in the government sphere.

The term Government Sponsored Enterprise (GSE) is often applied to so-called private enterprises that have been founded by government and still enjoy public support of one kind or another. Pre-eminent examples include the mortgage giants Fannie Mae and Freddie Mac. It is appropriate, however, to apply the term GSE more broadly to include:

- The defense industry (sells mostly to the government)
- Healthcare, drugs, housing, banking, finance, agriculture, food, autos, broadcasting, railroads, trucking, airlines, education (closely regulated, subsidized, price supported, protected, or cartelized by government)
- Law and accounting (expanded through government regulation and allowed to earn enormous fees in areas such as medical malpractice law)
- Unions (exempted from anti-trust law and favored in many other ways)
- Other niche organizations such as the American Association of Retired Persons (AARP) (which ostensibly exists to influence government, although it has become in effect a large business conglomerate aided and assisted by government)

It is clear enough why all these "private" firms and organizations reach out and try to ally themselves with public officials:

What Special Interests Want from Government

- Sales
- Favorable regulations

- Exemption from regulation
- Regulation that discourages new or small competitors
- Access to credit
- Access to cheap credit
- Loan guarantees
- Monopoly status
- Extension of monopoly status (patents and copyrights)
- Noncompetitive bidding or contracts
- Subsidies
- Bailouts
- Promise of a future bailout (which reduces current cost of credit)
- Protection from competitors, domestic or foreign
- Favorable price restrictions
- Targeted tax breaks

There is a quid pro quo for all this of course:

What Public Officials Want from Private Interests

- Campaign contributions
- Direct campaign assistance
- Indirect campaign assistance

- Assistance with "messaging"
- Money (illegal if a bribe, but not necessarily in other cases, e.g. assistance with a loan or access to a "sweetheart" investment)
- Support from "foundations" related to campaign contributors
- Regulatory fees to support agency jobs
- Jobs for friends, constituents, or eventually themselves
- Travel, entertainment, other "freebies"
- Power, control, and deference

After the 2008 Crash, commentator Michael Barone noted that many people expected US voters to turn against "Big Business" and "market solutions" in favor of more "Big Government."[73] But it is difficult to draw such distinctions when Big Business, Big Finance, Big Labor, Big Law, and Big Government all merge together into a single conglomerated entity, one that seems devoted to its own welfare rather than the public good.

Chapter Fourteen

The Progressive Paradox

I N THE PRIOR CHAPTERS, we noted that more government, and especially more government of the economy, produces the unintended consequence of more crony capitalism. This is an especially troublesome point for political progressives, who see more and bigger government as a way to control greedy private interests.

Senator Bernie Sanders, candidate for the Democratic Party presidential nomination in 2016, claimed in his speeches that:

> I am a proud progressive, prepared to stand with the working families of this country; prepared to take on powerful special interests which wield enormous power over the economic and political life of this country.[74]

What are we to make of this? Progressivism as a political movement began with one simple idea. Special interests comprised of rich people and corporations had too much power and were using it to the detriment of ordinary people. Progressives would deploy the power of government to regulate and quell these special interests. But there was a logical problem: the more government intervened in the economy, the more special interests sought to infiltrate government, which became increasingly corrupted.

Columnist George Will summarizes what might be called the progressive paradox as follows:

> [Progressives] have a rendezvous with regret. Their largest achievement is today's redistributionist government. But such government is inherently regressive: It tends to distribute power and money to the strong, including itself.

> Government becomes big by having big ambitions for supplanting markets as society's primary allocator of wealth and opportunity. Therefore it becomes a magnet for factions muscular enough, in money or numbers or both, to bend government to their advantage.[75]

The fifteenth to sixteenth-century Dutch philosopher and reformer Erasmus wrote that

> a city grows rich through the industry of its
> citizens only to be plundered by the greed
> of princes.[76]

This was not a complete account. When government plunders, it usually does so in alliance with powerful private interests, which may include prominent citizens or, in a democracy, strategic voter blocs, including voter blocs assembled on cultural as well as on economic grounds.

How then can government be expected to restrain the special interests with which it is closely allied? The more government "runs" the economy, the more private interests will insinuate themselves into politics and vice versa. Money and power will flow back and forth through ever more corrupted channels. Average citizens will always end up getting the short end of the stick, as they did during and after the Crash of 2008.

Progressive thinkers deal with this paradox in strikingly different ways. Some simply deny the problem. The *Economist* magazine, itself generally progressive, criticized leading progressive (and Keynesian) economist Joseph Stiglitz for taking the easy tack of denial:

> After [Stiglitz] has condemned today's
> policymakers so roundly as incompetent
> and beholden to special interests, [his] pre-
> scription [for] better regulation . . . and

> [his] broader faith in government activism sounds perverse. If policymakers failed as miserably as Mr. Stiglitz believes, then he ought to be far more worried about the potential for government failure in the future. That dissonance is a glaring weakness in Mr. Stiglitz's [position].[77]

Economist Bryan Caplan, discussing a book about crony capitalism by the "Marxist" historian Gabriel Kolko, similarly remarked that

> strange as it seems, [Kolko] sees the unholy alliance of business and government as an argument for government.[78]

Progressive economist Jeffrey Sachs at least acknowledges the paradox when he writes, in his book, *The Price of Civilization*, that

> yes, the federal government is incompetent and corrupt—but we need more, not less, of it.

This prompted Congressman Paul Ryan to respond, in a review, that Sach's position

> would be comical if it were not deadly serious.[79]

Some progressives are troubled by the illogic of their position and recognize the need for change. After all, is not a desire for change at the heart of progressivism? Is this not what the word is supposed to mean? Others have taken the opposite and (again paradoxical) stance of becoming reactionaries opposed to any change. Here is what Southern Methodist University (SMU) health policy analyst John Goodman said about progressive voters after the 2012 presidential election:

> If you are one of the folks who voted [as a progressive] in the last election, what did you vote for? ... Here are three things for starters: (1) no reform of the public schools, no reform of the welfare systems, and no reform of labor market institutions that erect barriers between new entrants and good jobs. ...
>
> The first three policies you voted for mean that those on the bottom rung of the income ladder are not going to get a helping hand to get on a higher rung. As far as those with the least income and wealth are concerned, you voted for status quo all the way. And to rub salt in the wound, the very people you voted for will be telling the world at every opportunity how much they care about the poor—even as they do everything to impede their economic mobility!
>
> Here are three more things you voted for: (1) no reform of the tax system, (2) no reform

of Social Security, Medicare, Medicaid and other entitlements, and (3) no serious effort to deal with mounting deficit spending and ever-increasing national debt. . . .

The second set of policies you voted for adds up to another bottom line: with respect to the nation's fiscal health, you voted again for status quo all the way. There is no mystery about the problem we face. We've promised more than we can afford. According to the Congressional Budget Office, if we continue on the path we are on the federal government will need to collect two-thirds of the income of the middle class and more than 90% of the income of high-income families by mid-century.

The idea of progressives as reactionaries will be an affront to most progressives, but where the shoe fits, they will have to wear it. Nor is it the most searing indictment. An even more disturbing idea is that many progressives, like many late twentieth century Soviet Communists, have lost their faith and, behind a mask of superficial pieties, are mainly focusing on what side their bread is buttered. On anything from a small to a large scale, they have become crony capitalists themselves.

People in this category include:

- Progressive teachers who mainly focus on getting higher pay or who talk up a lottery for education, even though lotteries just take money away from those who have the least;

- Progressive union members fighting for benefits at the expense of usually poorer non-union members, not to mention workers in other countries who may be desperately needy;

- Progressive seniors who do not mind being subsidized by young people who are on average the poorest group of all;

- Government workers who see themselves as serving their fellow citizens, especially those less advantaged, but who demand salaries, health insurance, and sometimes grossly inflated retirement benefits far in excess of what comparable workers in private industry earn and far beyond what taxes will support.

To see how far progressivism has fallen, we need only consult what John Gunther wrote about Progressivism in his book *Inside USA*, published in 1946:

> The age of the Pleistocene marauders and despoilers has passed . . . , is as dead as Tutankhamen. . . . The permanent, durable ground swell is progressive. . . . This is a country that believes in two things above all—progress and reform.[80]

But even Gunther worried about "selling out to the big interests who were originally the opposition," and given the weaknesses of human nature and the imperfectability of government officials, he had reason to worry.[81]

Today the children of the confident and committed reformers may be talking the old progressive talk, but they seem to have found a comfortable spot in the crony capitalist system. They have traveled a long distance from what may have been the idealism of their youth, still mirrored in the young people who intensely protest against what they call "capitalism," communicating through their iPhones, digging up information on the internet with iPads, or meeting up at Starbucks to recharge with very costly varieties of caffeine, all with little or no perceived irony, but at least with a still untainted sincerity.

The essence of the problem with all these versions of progressivism was partly captured by investor and author Jim Rogers when he wrote that:

> Governments are terrible at engendering prosperity and wealth.[82]

But it must be added that their efforts to create prosperity and wealth more often than not create corruption, and nothing is more deadly for sustained prosperity than corruption.

However well-intentioned progressive ideas of government leading the economy may be, they always entail dismantling of the price system, and this will not work. By now this should be clear enough. Endlessly repeating the errors of the recent past will just make things worse, much worse. Treasury Secretary Henry Morgenthau, President Franklin Roosevelt's close friend and heartfelt progressive, admitted in 1939 that government leadership of the economy had not rescued us from the Great Depression:

> I want to see this country prosperous. I want to see people get enough to eat. We have never made good on our promises. . . . I say after eight years of this administration we have just as much unemployment as when we started and an enormous debt to boot.[83]

Walter Lippmann, another famous progressive who believed deeply in the promise of government economic leadership, finally agreed in 1943 that it tended to produce the opposite of what was intended:

> This is the vicious paradox of the gradual collectivism which has developed in western society during the past sixty years: it has provoked the expectation of universal plenty provided by action of the state while, through almost every action undertaken or tolerated by the state, the production of wealth is restricted.[84]

The customary progressive response to Lippmann's plaintive observation is that we just need an even stronger dose of the same medicine. But this defies logic. Lippmann was reporting on sixty years of free price destruction; we have had almost seventy more years since. It is time to face reality and move on.

Some progressives try to distract themselves and others from these economic failures by refocusing progressivism on cultural issues. But the economic issues cannot be avoided. Even if one espouses "multiculturalism" and "diversity" (as currently defined by contemporary progressives along racial or gender lines rather than, for example, diversity of opinion), how can it be advanced in a failing and increasingly corrupt economy?

Intellectual revolutions are always hard fought, and the fighting takes a long time to play out. Social and economic establishments are determined to preserve their privilege. At first they mock their critics; any argument for reform, however factual or logical, is greeted with derision. What a joke! Once it becomes clear that the other side is making its case and starting to gain a foothold with the voting public, mockery is succeeded by stony silence. Everything the critics say is now ignored, lest more people hear about it. In the next stage, the established elite finally acknowledges its critics and comes out battling, using every device at hand to try to destroy them. If this fails, and the critics finally win the battle of public opinion, the old elite simply says: "Oh, we knew that all along."

Today the progressive elites are feeling besieged. They are no longer just mocking their critics. They are finding it more and more difficult to ignore them. The third stage battle seems to have been joined, with the final result still to be seen.

Chapter Fifteen

Where Does This Leave the Poor?

I T IS IMPOSSIBLE to say how many people are poor in the United States and elsewhere. Government statistics often intentionally obscure the facts. For example, in the United States the biggest federal poverty program, the Earned Income Tax Credit (EITC), pays 27 million taxpayers $60 billion in cash. But like Section 8 housing vouchers and Medicaid, EITC payments are excluded when the government totes up who is poor and who is not.

Moreover, since the Crash of 2008, more and more formerly middle-class people have slipped into a state of near poverty. For example, they can no longer afford to buy a reliable automobile, and without a reliable automobile find their employment options limited not only by the economy, but also by transportation barriers. In addition, they may own a home that cannot find a buyer, which means they cannot easily move to another state with more jobs.

There is supposed to be a "social safety net" for the truly poor, an array of government programs that was greatly expanded after the Crash of 2008. Of that "net," GOP candidate Mitt Romney said during the 2012, presidential campaign:

> I'm not concerned about the very poor. We have a safety net there. If it needs repair, I'll fix it.[85]

Can there really be any doubt that it needs fixing? A Senate subcommittee found that the US government in 2012 was making "welfare" payments equivalent to $168 per day for every household whose income fell below the official poverty line. Since median income of all Americans is $137 a day, it is clear that only a small part of the $168 (equivalent to about $36,000 a year) is actually reaching the poor.

Much of the money is going to other people, including government workers who, supported by powerful public unions, are indirect but prime beneficiaries of poverty programs. Looking at all government transfer payments, not just those included in the congressional study, a study suggests that only 36% of the money goes to the bottom 20% of earners and even less to the truly poor.[86] The greater part of the money goes to households headed by 65-year-olds or older whose net worth is a stunning 47 times greater than households headed by under 35-year-olds.[87]

Another feature of the welfare spending is that it does not just create disincentives to work. It actually taxes work at a far higher rate than that applied through the regular tax code. As economist Thomas Sowell has pointed out, a low-income individual may find that the next $10,000 of earned income will reduce federal benefits by $15,000, which in effect represent a 150% "tax" rate.[88] This is completely unfair, but remains largely unacknowledged, much less addressed, by public policy.

When thinking about welfare spending, we should also ask: where does the money come from? In part, it comes from taxes paid by higher income earners. But much of it is borrowed. When the time comes to pay the interest or repay the debt, who will receive the money—rich or poor? It will be the rich of course, either rich Americans or rich foreigners or foreign central banks. It will not be the poor.

Other government policies do not make things better. The federal minimum wage was raised in steps to $7.25 during and after the Crash of 2008. This hurt impoverished, inexperienced young workers the most, so why would anyone be surprised that the teenage unemployment rate rose to 26% in 2009, 39% for black teenagers, and 52% for all teenagers in Washington, DC?

Obamacare, President Obama's signature and mandatory medical insurance program, compounded this problem by adding $2.28–$5.89 of cost per hour for every full-time worker and more for part-time. How can an uneducated worker gain the experience and track record needed to earn such wages without work? And yet how can he or she get the work with such mandated wages? If they are lucky, teenagers work today as "interns" for nothing. Why not at least allow a "training wage," so that idle teenagers could both learn and earn?

Obamacare also encouraged the creation of Accountable Care Organizations, where medical professionals were to be paid for health "outcomes" rather than on a fee for service basis. Because low-income patients tend to have worse "outcomes," ACOs were almost guaranteed over time to minimize the number of such patients. And who would decide the definition of a "good" outcome in the first place?

Under market conditions, consumers ultimately choose what is "good" or "bad" at a given price. By doing so, they also define what "healthcare" is. If the government defines "healthcare," it will ultimately be decided by the strongest special interests, including the American Medical Association, the big hospitals, big insurance and drug companies, and other players.

There is an even more basic problem for the poor. Each year, the price of everything increases. In part, the price increases are directly caused by government rules and mandates. Recently, the federal government required the installation of a "black box" in each automobile, which will give speed (and other potentially incriminating information) in the event of a crash. Like other government requirements, this will increase the price of a car, making it that much harder for the poor to buy one.

The "cash for clunkers" program created after the Crash of 2008 was supposed to assist both the automobile companies and low-income buyers, and to reduce car pollution as well. It mostly produced a lot of unintended consequences. First, it greatly reduced used car supply, so that those prices rose, shutting out poor buyers. Second, it resulted in many poor quality loans that were followed by repossession. The buyer had lost his or her used car and now had no car at all. And, finally, it led to more air pollution, not less, because of the way that car disposal rules were written. Parts that could have been recycled were not, for fear of cheating, but were instead incinerated.

Government licensing requirements raise the cost of even the most basic services for the poor. Hair-cutting costs more, because employees are not allowed to learn by doing, but must take expensive, prescribed courses. Childcare costs much more because the neighbor down the street is no longer allowed to take your children for the day in return for a payment. These rules are all introduced as consumer protections, but more often than not protect cartels of service providers, and invariably raise prices, which hurts the poor most directly. Even the ability of the poor to escape the ghetto is impeded by rules against "gypsy" car services. And when local and state governments keep expanding to create and enforce these rules, the sales taxes may go up, which also hit the poor hardest.

As important as all these price elevators are, they are not the chief way that government raises prices for the poor. As we have pointed out in earlier chapters, the free price system tends to drive down prices, while incontinent federal money creation keeps driving them up.

This is not especially hard on the rich. They generally know how to protect themselves or even turn the inflation to their advantage by making shrewd investments in sectors where the new money created by the Fed is blowing up bubbles. Meanwhile the middle class and the poor must work harder and harder to afford the same standard of living or, more likely, face a declining standard of living.

There is no lack of excuses for what inflation does to the poor. Alan Blinder, vice-chairman of the Fed under President Bill Clinton, says that the harm [which] inflation inflicts on the economy is often exaggerated.[89]

Blinder seems to think that lowering interest rates by printing more money will increase economic growth, that this will help the poor and reduce income inequality, and that inflation is a small price to pay for these gains. But none of this is actually true. Thwarting free prices, relentlessly and mindlessly interfering with interest rates and currencies in particular, leads to chronic instability and job destruction. Rising prices just add further to the miseries of the poor, as numerous studies have shown.[90] Domingo Cavallo, Finance Minister of Argentina in the 1990s, was right when he stated that the poor are the foremost victims of inflation, followed only by the middle class.

A variant of Blinder's argument has been voiced by Christina Romer, President Obama's first Chairman of the Council of Economic Advisors. Money printing, she says

> tends to lower the price of the dollar [which is] good for ordinary families.[91]

The basic idea here is that consumer goods from China will be cheaper. What this ignores is that other countries will print just as much or more money in response, de facto currency devaluations will escalate endlessly, and, again, bubble and bust will follow, producing mainly unemployment and suffering for the poor.

Moreover, the very poorest of the poor will not be able to afford even the cheap imported goods. They will not even be able to afford to travel to a mall. They will be lucky if food is sold anywhere near where they live, and if it is, the price will likely be higher than elsewhere because of security risks for the store owner and lack of competition. If they are lucky enough to have a job, nothing they produce is likely to be exported and thus benefit from a wider market. All of this is equally true for the American slum dweller as for a poor and isolated Asian farmer.

If the poor are able to buy imported goods, the things they need will probably have a higher tariff attached to them than the luxury goods intended for the rich. This is true in almost every country. For example, a study by the Progressive Policy Institute in the US showed that imported goods bought by poor or middle-class people (e.g., clothes and shoes) had an average tariff of 10.5% versus an average tariff of only 0.8% on luxury goods.[92] Tariffs are not only a tax, albeit a hidden tax; they are a peculiarly regressive tax.

If we are at all serious about ending poverty, much less improving the plight of the poor, we need to acknowledge the utter perversity of what we are doing today, and find a new way forward. Instead of focusing mostly on the gap between rich and poor, that is, relative poverty, we should focus more on absolute poverty, on getting people to a safe and reasonably comfortable standard of living that opens up choices and opportunities. There is not that much difference between having enough money and having an infinite amount of it. The goal should be to get everyone to "enough." Government policy should support this by leaving prices free to do their job, not thwart it with toxic price manipulations and controls.

Chapter Sixteen

How the Fed Fits In

A s we saw in Lesson Two, a free price system drives consumer prices down, not up. It gives us a gradual reduction in prices, exactly what we should want. Falling consumer prices are the payoff for learning to produce goods and services more and more productively.

Innovation and productivity, along with accompanying consumer price reductions, define economic progress. They are especially helpful to the poor, who can buy more and more with limited means. For everyone, but especially for the poor, rising prices are a threat, and also an admission of economic failure.

For most of the decades prior to the founding of the United States Federal Reserve, US prices fluctuated but ended up where they started. A loaf of bread cost no more at the dawn of the twentieth century than it had during the Revolutionary War. Two years after the US Federal Reserve began operation in 1914, consumer price inflation soared. Since the Fed was charged with controlling inflation, this was not a good harbinger for the future. Thereafter prices tended to peak and crater, but mostly rose.

As the Fed's first century passed, the dollar had lost a stunning 97% of its purchasing power, 90% just from 1950. By 2014, a consumer needed $33 to buy what one dollar would have bought in 1914. Millionaires, defined as people with a net worth of $1 million dollars, were no longer even classed as "rich."

Fed Chairman Paul Volcker, who was deservedly admired and had temporarily beaten back inflation during his tenure, conceded that:

> If the overriding objective is price stability, we did a better job with the nineteenth-century gold standard . . . or even [with]"free banking."[93]

After Volcker, government statistics about the rate of inflation also became increasingly unreliable, especially during and after the Clinton administration. The changes tended to depress the reported number, which also served to reduce Social Security payments owed by the government. Without these changes, the reported loss of purchasing power since the founding of the Fed would look much worse.

Why and how has this happened? To get to the bottom of this question, we must first ask what causes consumer price inflation. A popular idea is that prices rise when an economy grows too fast and becomes "overheated." But economic growth means that more goods and services are being produced. This increase in supply, as noted previously, should tend to reduce, not increase prices.

By far the most important reason that prices rise and stay high is that government has "printed"* new money and injected it into the economy—either directly or through the banking system. As the amount of money circulating rises relative to the supply of goods and services, the price of those goods and services expressed in dollars naturally rises.

A simple example may help make this clear. If the economy consisted entirely of two knives and $2, it would be logical for each knife to be priced at $1. But if the amount of money doubles to $4, without any more knives being produced, the price of each of the two existing knives would be expected to rise to $2. Economist Milton Friedman summed this up in a famous passage:

---

* This refers to electronic means of creating money, not just printing of paper bills.

> Just as an excessive increase in the quan-
> tity of money is the one and only impor-
> tant cause of inflation, so a reduction in the
> rate of monetary growth is the one and only
> cure for inflation.[94]

This is not entirely true. Consumer expectations about the amount of money that will be created drives consumer price inflation even more than the actual amount that has been created, but the two are closely linked, so Friedman's point is still valid. The Federal Reserve is responsible for and in many ways seeks to control the quantity of money in the US. It therefore follows that the Fed is responsible for the dollar's collapse in purchasing power since 1914.

Looking more closely at the dollar's loss of purchasing power, 90% was lost just since 1950, and most of that since 1971, when the last link of the dollar to gold reserves was severed by the Nixon administration. The requirement of maintaining some gold reserve backing the dollar had acted as a brake, however weak, on dollar creation. Ironically, one of the framers of the Federal Reserve Act, Senator Elihu Root, had considered making a 100% gold-backed dollar part of the legislation, but concluded it was unnecessary. He told colleagues the US government would never dare to issue paper currency backed by nothing. The framers of the Constitution, including Alexander Hamilton, had assumed the same.

As Hamilton pointed out in a letter,* the problem with US dollars backed by nothing is that the government can create as many of them as it wishes, without any restraint at all, which is exactly what it did after 1971. And an unrestrained flood of new dollars will eventually undermine the economy, either by creating too much debt, or by setting off hyperinflation, either in consumer prices or asset prices or both.

Hamilton did not object to private banks issuing notes that were the equivalent of paper money. That was different, because it could be regulated by market forces. If a private bank overdid it: "It will return upon the bank."[95]

---

* Hamilton wanted a central bank, but he specifically warned against governments or central banks printing paper money, as they do today:

> The emitting of paper money by the authority of Government is wisely prohibited. . . . Though paper emissions, under a general authority, might have some advantage . . . yet they are of a nature so liable to abuse—and it may even be affirmed, so certain of being abused—that the wisdom of the Government will be shown in never trusting itself with the use of so seducing and dangerous an expedient. . . . The stamping of paper is an operation so much easier than the laying of taxes, that a government, in the practice of paper emissions, would rarely fail . . . to indulge itself too far in the employment of that resource . . . even to [the point of creating] . . . an absolute bubble. [Alexander Hamilton, Report to the House of Representatives, December 13, 1790, in American State Papers, Finance, 1st Congress, 3rd Session, no. 18, I, 67–76; also quoted in Jude Wanniski, *The Way the World Works: How Economies Fail—and Succeed* (New York: Basic Books, 1978), 204–5.]

Chapter Seventeen

The Fed's Conflict
of Interest

I T IS ASKING for malfeasance to have a government financier able to create money at will. It is a fantasy to think that any institution can centrally plan an economy. To combine these roles in the same institution also represents a truly massive and destructive conflict of interest. It is an invitation for the government to do whatever it believes will best serve its short-term interests, such as paying off friends and getting through the next election, rather than what will serve the long-term interests of the nation. And it is an invitation that government officials have readily accepted.

Financier

Since the Fed was created by an act of Congress, why does Congress not step in to reform the agency? Thibault de Saint Phalle, author of *The Federal Reserve: An Intentional Mystery*, explains that:

> No one in Congress ever points out . . . it is the Fed itself that creates inflation. [The reason for this is that] the Fed, by financing the federal deficit year after year, makes it possible for Congress to continue to spend far more than it collects in tax revenues. If it were not for Fed action, Congress would have to curb its spending habits dramatically.[96]

What exactly does de Saint Phalle mean by this? How does the Fed help finance government deficit spending when it creates new money? In most cases, this is done indirectly.

The government borrows money by selling a bond, let us say to a bank. The Federal Reserve then buys the bond from the bank with newly "printed" money. In effect, the government sells a bond to itself, but very few people understand what is happening.

Most people believe that the largest creditors of the US government, buyers of its bonds, are the Japanese and Chinese governments. This is not correct. The largest owner of US government bonds is the US government itself, operating through the Federal Reserve.

A government is expected to finance itself through taxes. Historically, governments hard up for money have also created new currency to spend. In the 1920s, Germany simply printed new marks. If a central bank buys in a government bond, it is the functional equivalent of printing new currency. Whatever the method—taxes, currency printing, or buying in bonds—the result is to transfer resources from the private sector to government.

To see this more clearly, assume that an economy consists of $1 and miscellaneous goods and services. Government may either levy 25¢ in taxes or "print" 33.3¢ in new money for its own use. Either way government now has the wherewithal to command 25% of all economy-wide goods and services. (25¢ is a quarter of $1.00 and 33.3¢ is a quarter of $1.00 plus 33.3¢.) Private businesses and individuals are left with 75%.

Even if governments do not create money in order to finance their own deficits directly, an expansion of the money supply will still enable them to borrow more. This is because rising consumer prices steadily reduce the real value of the debt. If I lend $1,000 to anyone, the borrower gets $1,000 in purchasing power. If the borrower repays me after twenty years, and there has been inflation of a little over 3.5% a year in the interim, I only get back $500 in purchasing power.

The US government is fully aware that inflation allows the borrower to slip out of contractual debt without default. As federal debt exploded following the Crash of 2008, it became clear that the Bernanke Fed hoped to inflate away the massive debt, but to do so slowly enough to avoid setting off alarms among lenders, which could lead to a bond buyer strike and spiraling interest rates.

Central Planner

In 1977, Congress gave the Fed an additional mandate: bring down unemployment. This enabled the Fed to regard itself as our national economic planner. This was done even though The Fed's creation of new dollars was the single leading contributor to economic bubbles (followed by crashes) in the late 1910s and 1920s, before the new mandate, as well as during the late 1990s and 2000s, after the new authority was in place. Even after these calamities, textbooks and media commentators still pretend that the Fed helps stabilize the economy. Economic writer Jeffrey Madrick wrote after the Crash of 2008:

> By 1913, the US federal government created a stable financial system with the creation of the Federal Reserve.[97]

This was runaway wishful thinking.

Economist Milton Friedman got it right again when he said that

> The severity of each of the major economic contractions . . . is directly attributable to acts of . . . the Reserve authorities and would not have occurred under earlier monetary and banking arrangements.[98]

Note that Friedman wrote this in 1962, long before the Fed-provoked calamities of the 1970s inflation or the bubbles and crashes of the 1990s and 2000s.

About all this, respected economic writer James Grant writes:

> Central planning may be discredited in the broader sense, but people still believe in central planning as it is practiced by . . . [the Fed]. . . . To my mind the Fed is a cross between the late, unlamented Interstate Commerce Commission and the Wizard of Oz.[99]

Economist William Anderson compares the Fed and its leaders to Gosplan, the agency charged with preparing economic plans for the Soviet Union, and thinks that it has the same chance of success. Economic writer Gene Callahan gets to the heart of the matter when he writes that the chairman of the Federal Reserve "is the head price fixer of a price fixing agency."[100]

Why price fixer? This is correct because the Fed uses its control of money to fix some interest rates and manipulate others, and interest rates are among the most important prices of the economy.

Ironically, former Fed chairman Ben Bernanke told a university economics class that:

> Prices are the thermostat of an economy. They are the mechanisms by which an economy functions.[101]

Most economists agree that price controls destroy an economy. But, like Bernanke and Yellen, they often wear blinders which prevent them from seeing that everything the Fed does is a price control.

The Fed also decided that the 1977 expansion of its mandate authorized it to manipulate the stock market and housing as well as the bond and money markets, an expansion of mission that has not helped the economy. At the same time, the Fed has not always paid close attention to the statute governing its mission. Although much of what it did during and after the Crash of 2008 was legal, some of it was illegal, in particular buying Fannie and Freddie mortgage-backed securities. This was later addressed by amending the statute, but not before the illegal activity took place on a massive scale.

The Fed record of failure for a century speaks for itself, but the prognostications of Fed leaders are not any more reassuring. Former Fed chairman Ben

Bernanke had an almost unbroken record of being wrong, although he was almost matched by his vice chairman, then successor, Janet Yellen. In 2006, at the zenith of the greatest housing bubble in history, Bernanke told Congress that house prices would continue to rise. In 2007, he testified that failing sub-prime mortgages would not threaten the economy. In January 2008, at a luncheon, he told his audience there was no recession on the horizon. As late as July 2008, he insisted that mortgage giants Fannie Mae and Freddie Mac, already teetering on the verge of collapse, were "adequately capitalized [and] in no danger of failing."[102]

Following the Crash of 2008, Bernanke's and then Yellen's Fed embarked on the most radical monetary experiment in US history. It responded to a crisis caused by too much new money and debt, by engineering an even greater flood of new money and debt. Harvard economist Ken Rogoff accurately summed it up by saying: "We borrowed too much, we screwed up, so we're going to fix it by borrowing more."[103] (Ironically, Rogoff actually favored the policy; he just wanted an even more radical version of it.)

In the face of criticism, neither the Fed leaders nor any of its allied Keynesian economists ever bothered to offer logical or factual arguments explaining how this approach of creating ever more new money and piling new debt on top of bad old debt could possibly work. At her Senate confirmation hearings, Janet Yellen offered this classic example of Fed doublespeak:

> If we want to get back to business as usual and a normal monetary policy and normal interest rates, I would say we need to do that by getting the economy back to normal.

How informative! Yellen brushed off an observation by Senator Mike Johanns (R-NE) that Fed stimulus is putting the economy on an unsustainable "sugar high," or a similar reference by Senator Pat Toomey (R-PA) to the monetary "morphine drip" the Fed has been administering.

At a later Congressional hearing, Yellen reported that "progress on price stability has been notably absent."[104] In her Orwellian double speak, the word stability actually meant consumer price inflation. Translated, this meant that the agency charged by law with preventing consumer price inflation had sought to increase it but its efforts had failed.

A number of highly respected economists have concluded that the Fed's post-Crash of 2008 new money creation backfired even in purely Keynesian terms, the terms in which the Fed itself thought. Lower interest rates were intended to increase borrowing and spending and thus economic "demand." But that turned out to count for less than the lost demand from lenders earning little or no interest. Moreover, banks chose to hold back from lending when rates were artificially low and expected to rise.

Even a largely sympathetic observer, Mohammed El-Arian, former CEO of the giant bond manager PIMCO, estimated that Fed's activities added as little as $40 billion to economic output or ¼ of one percent of GDP in the first four years after the Crash. Other economists thought the contribution was negative.

The Fed insisted that it could reverse all the new money it had conjured up anytime it wished. Ben Bernanke said on *60 Minutes* that he was 100% confident of being able to do so. But respected economist John Hussman called Fed's post-2008 policies a "roach motel, easy to get into but hard to get out of." He calculated that raising short-term interest rates back to 2%, a very low rate by historical standards, would have required the Fed to sell at least $1.5 trillion of securities on the open market. Who would buy those securities?

Since World War II, the US government has counted on foreign central banks to buy US treasuries not purchased by the Fed. These foreign central banks, like the Fed, are using newly created money. But their willingness to hold more US debt has sharply waned in recent years. Some foreign central banks, including China's and Russia's, appear to be openly hostile to the current global monetary system in which the US dollar has special reserve status. They want to replace it.

The fear of not finding buyers for federal bonds, with a subsequent collapse of the federal bond market, may be exactly what triggered the Fed's radical actions in the face of the 2008 crisis. The Fed may have done what it did, not to rescue Main Street, as it said, but to rescue Wall Street, with the understanding that Wall Street would thereby be able to keep buying more government bonds itself. It is illegal for the Fed to buy bonds directly from the government with its newly created money. It needs Wall Street as an intermediary to buy the bonds before selling them back to the Fed. If this sounds like a shell game, it is because it is a shell game.

The Fed invented the term "quantitative easing" to describe its favored method of creating trillions of new dollars following the 2008 Crash. Mainstream media commentators add to the confusion by calling it "bond buying," deliberately omitting the pertinent fact that the "bond buying" was done with money created out of thin air. Other, even more radical policies were developed for possible future use.

Chapter Eighteen

Who Exactly Is Feeding off the Fed?

WALL STREET PROFITS from the Fed's proclivity to "print" more and more new money in many ways. Most of this new money passes through Wall Street on its way to wherever it is going in the economy, and in transit fattens Wall Street bonuses. In addition, although some of the money enters the consumer economy, where it raises consumer prices, much of it enters investment markets, where it raises the prices of stock, bonds, or real estate. Wall Street generally benefits from rising asset prices, as well as from all the speculation triggered by the new money.

Managers of big corporations also benefit from Fed maneuvers. The massive deficits of the federal government that are financed by the Fed boost corporate profits. This is why, in the aftermath of the Crash of 2008, historically very high corporate profits existed right alongside glacial economic growth and high unemployment. Indeed, the high unemployment helped to keep wages low, so that profits were further boosted by low wage costs.

It got even better for corporate insiders. They could also borrow the Fed's newly printed money at negligible rates, and use the proceeds of the loans to buy in company stock. This was supposed to help shareholders by increasing earnings per share, but really helped the managers and other insiders offset and render invisible the stock dilution caused by their own cheap share options awards. Share repurchases also helped keep the share price high, so that the options would be valuable when exercised.

In sharp contrast, average people do not benefit from any of this, quite the contrary. They do not own many investment assets to protect themselves from inflation. If poor, they may own none at all. They just lose their jobs or raises during the busts that follow the bubbles. If they are lucky enough to be able to think about buying a car or house, they find that the costs keep rising, especially in relation to their income.

As has been widely noted, US workers' wages have been stagnant or falling in real (inflation-adjusted terms) for many years. But it is the future of worker's wages that is especially bleak. Ask yourself a simple question. Why are US workers paid more than those in most other countries? The answer is that they are more productive.

And why are they more productive? Partly because they are better educated, although that advantage is eroding. A more important difference is that American workers have more investment capital behind them—capital that has been put in place precisely to increase productivity or improve quality. Note, however, that as the Fed prints new money, and companies borrow to buy in their stock, the one thing they are not doing is investing in the new plant and equipment needed to pay for the future wage gains of workers.

American consumers and companies have saved and invested in recent decades, although at a reduced rate compared to history. And much of that has been lost in fruitless bubbles that came and went. Too much of what remains consists of bubble assets or firms that should have been liquidated, but have instead been propped up by bailouts or crony-ridden regulations.

By now, what the government calls private gross domestic investment is actually lower than in the late 1990s. At this rate, American workers are living on borrowed time, because they are using older, no longer cutting-edge capital. How long will it take developing countries to overtake our wages, either because US wages fall or other countries' wages rise? That completely depends on whether the US stops relying on the Fed's toxic money printing presses and instead starts to save and invest—not only save and invest, but invest wisely in legitimate, well-chosen equipment and enterprises.

No one really benefits from our present Fed-financed crony capitalist world. Even the seeming beneficiaries—government, Wall Street, big corporations—are just sowing the seeds of their own future destruction. In the meantime, however, it is the middle-class, and the poor most of all, who pay the price.

Looking back at the lamentable record of the Fed over a century and especially in recent decades, economist Marc Faber concluded that the concatenation of so many misjudgments and policy errors would eventually lead to demands for the dethronement of central bankers as national economic planners:

> When . . . the public . . . finally realizes that central bankers are no wiser than the central planners of former communist regimes, the tide will turn and monetary reform will come to the fore. . . . At that time . . . market forces [will again] drive economic activity, and not some kind of central planner: regardless whether they stand forth as senior officials of totalitarian regimes—or come cleverly disguised as central bankers.[105]

Chapter Nineteen

Keynes's *General Theory*: The Crony Bible*

T HE FEDERAL RESERVE at one time in its history was staffed by people drawn from finance and business. Today it is almost entirely staffed by PhD economists from universities. Virtually all of these in turn are political progressives whose economic views have been shaped by the British economist John Maynard Keynes (1883–1946).

Keynes's principal book, *The General Theory of Employment, Interest, and Money*, occupies the same

---

* For more information, see the author's *Where Keynes Went Wrong* (Mt. Jackson, VA: Axios Press, 2009).

place in progressivism that Karl Marx's *Capital* occupies in communism. One is the "sacred text," obscure enough to require "priestly" interlocutors, the other the actual social system, although it could be argued that Keynes's system may be more accurately described, not as progressivism, but as crony capitalism. This interpretation of Keynesianism as the bible for crony capitalism is supported by Keynes's own explicit admission in *The General Theory* that he was reviving the thinking of mercantilists, early economists from the sixteenth and seventeenth centuries who were unabashed apologists for the crony capitalism of their day.

Long after his death, Keynes is still the best-known expositor of today's conventional economic wisdom: the doctrine that economies, especially faltering economies, should be "stimulated" by governments printing new money, driving down interest rates, borrowing the new money back, spending, and when necessary bailing out powerful private interests, although the latter step reflects contemporary Keynesians Alan Greenspan and Ben Bernanke more than Keynes himself. Keynes had wrongly assumed that driving down interest rates alone would suffice to pull the US out of the Great Depression.

Keynesianism is replete with vivid paradoxes. A weak economy caused by an alleged glut of savings can be cured by creating more "savings," which is what he called newly printed money. A problem of too much debt can similarly be solved with more debt. Saving and investment were not, as generally thought, the road to wealth. Spending, not saving, makes us rich. Nor do high interest rates encourage savers and saving. Low rates supposedly produce more saving, although, since more saving is undesirable, the prescription of lower and lower rates seems doubly paradoxical.

When confronted by intractable economic problems, Keynes liked to offer big, dramatic ideas, but he also liked what he called

"tricks,"[106]

ingenious technical solutions that no one else would have contemplated or dared suggest. Confronted with the failure of Keynesian policies either to prevent the Crash of 2008 or to cure its aftermath, and especially confronted with the plague of crony capitalism that has accompanied the expansion of government leadership of the economy on Keynesian lines, some of Keynes's disciples have responded with some proposed "tricks" of their own. In each instance, the gist of the advice is that government should double down by taking an even larger role in running the economy and influencing or controlling prices. Two of these proposals include:

- Accelerate creation of new money to drive up consumer price index inflation, perhaps to as high as 6%. Meanwhile continue to control interest rates, holding short rates to near zero, by using the new money to buy securities. The idea is to encourage new borrowing and spending by virtually giving money away at—6% real (inflation-adjusted) rates. (Gregory Mankiw, Harvard).[107]

- Develop a desired level of borrowing (and spending) for the economy each year, and then take whatever actions would guarantee that this level is reached. (George Akerlof, UC, Berkeley, and Robert, Yale).[108]

Other proposals include the following:

- Raise taxes on employers and those holding jobs and use the proceeds to encourage hiring, in particular by subsidizing $4.50 of each new low-income worker's wage. (Robert Shiller, Yale).[109]

- Issue new government securities that will never be repaid. (Robert Shiller, Yale).[110] Of course, the government already issues debt that it does not expect to repay, just roll over into new debt, forever into the future, but this would acknowledge that the debt would never be repaid.

- Call on workers and employers to reduce wages by 7.5%, use the proceeds to hire new workers, and repay the existing workers with company stock or future profit sharing equal to the 7.5% of wages they gave up. (Lawrence Kotlikoff, Boston University, 2011).[111]

- Put economists in charge of deciding which industries have prices and wages that are too high, then intervene to reduce them. (Kotlikoff, 2011).

- Compel or persuade everyone to take an uncompensated 10% pay cut, with employers putting all this money into new hiring. (Ken Mayland, president, Clear View Economics).[112]

- Set taxes so that the income of the top 1% of households will never be more than 36x the median household income. Everything above that level would be taxed away. (Ian Ayres, Yale, and Aaron S. Edlin, UC, Berkeley).[113]

- [If additional monetary stimulus is needed], abolish paper money, replace it with electronic accounts that will be subject to a reverse rate of interest to encourage spending, and use newly printed money to buy assets other than government securities, in order to overcome

  > institutional conservatism, [and] a lack of coordination and cooperation between monetary and fiscal authorities due to a range of political dysfunctionalities. (Willem Buiter and Ebrahim Rahbari, Citigroup economists).[114]

- In the case of the Bank of Japan, which has previously used newly printed money to "buy" government bonds, it should print even more money and use it to "buy"

> physical assets such as real estate, . . . airports, sports stadiums, rice farms, dormant nuclear reactors, golf courses, universities, entire villages . . . , you name it . . . get creative. (William Pesek, economic writer based in Tokyo).[115]

Rather than follow Keynes and his followers down all these rabbit holes, let us ask ourselves: are there some common themes to these schemes? And there are. The first common theme is that market prices do not matter. No free price or profit relationship should be left alone. The price/profit system should be pulled completely apart and left to economists to try to reassemble it in some fashion.

And what about crony capitalism? How will all these schemes help rein in the corruption that just deepens as the government dismantles the free price system? We do not hear this question even being asked, much less answered. Robert Skidelsky, ardent Keynesian and author of a definitive three-volume Keynes biography, says that

> The system of the past 30 years . . . has . . . benefit[ed] a predatory plutocracy that creams off the riches.[116]

Well, yes. But what he completely fails to notice is how complicit Keynesianism is in the creation of this corrupt crony capitalist system.

Chapter Twenty

Saying Goodbye to Crony Capitalism

ANY SYSTEMIC AND SUCCESSFUL REFORM of crony capitalism will take government out of the business of influencing, manipulating, or controlling market prices. The crony capitalist system depends on these price manipulations; they are what private interests buy and what public officials sell. Crony capitalism will wither without them. As it withers, corruption will subside. The economy will recover and thrive. Jobs will once again be available for those able to work. Free prices must therefore be the banner under which today's reformers march.

It is not just a paradoxical doctrine that the economy can be improved by destroying the price mechanism on which it depends. It is an utterly false doctrine. It is time to restore free prices.

As we noted earlier, Ben Bernanke, chairman of the Fed during the Crash of 2008, agrees that "prices are the thermostat of an economy . . . , the mechanism . . . by which an economy functions,"[117] but he nevertheless radically expanded the price fixing reach of the Fed from short-term interest rates to all kinds of interest rates, among other radical unsuccessful experiments.

The federal government, supported and financed by the Fed, has steadily expanded its own price manipulations, monopolies, and subsidies. The mindset is always the same. When Obamacare was passed, a direct price control feature was added to the many indirect price controls for future use. Many state governments have done the same: Massachusetts amended its "Romneycare universal health plan" by passing a medical price control law in 2012, a law that requires government approval not only of price changes, but of every single "material" change by healthcare providers.[118] In each case, price controls are expanded as a remedy for ills created in the first place by earlier price controls. In the process, medical innovation, price reduction, and choice are destroyed.

These are obvious examples, but on close examination almost everything the government does in trying to nudge or lead the economy involves a price manipulation or control. It is time to pay heed to some sensible advice from humorist P. J. O'Rourke:

> [The free price system] is a bathroom scale.
> We may not like what we see when we step
> on the bathroom scale, but we can't pass
> a law making ourselves weigh 165 . . . ."[119]

To which O'Rourke adds:

> Bringing the government in to run . . . [eco-
> nomics] is like saying, "Dad burned dinner,
> let's get the dog to cook."[120]

A thriving economy is comprised of billions of prices
and trillions of price relationships. Left alone, these
prices almost miraculously coordinate demand with
supply so that buyers can obtain as much as possible of
what they want. Refusing to let prices fall or pushing
them higher (2% a year, now 2 .5% a year, per the Fed's
announced target, linked to an artificial and dubious
index) is like jamming a stick into the spokes of a wheel
or pouring sand into the fuel tank of an engine. If we do
this, we should not wonder if the wheel ceases to turn or
the engine refuses to run.

A successful society is a cooperative society. A cooperative society is an honest society. By far the most reliable barometer of economic honesty is to be found in
prices. Honest prices, neither manipulated nor controlled, provide both investors and consumers with
reliable economic signals. A corrupt, crony capitalist
economic system does not want honest prices, honest

information, or honest results. The truth may be inconvenient or unprofitable for powerful government leaders or private interests allied with them.

We need to allow prices to tell the truth, free from the self-dealing and self-interested theories that stand in their way. Any proposed government action in the economy should be evaluated on this one criterion at least: does it confuse, manipulate, or control prices? If it does, it should be rejected.

Is it possible that this one reform proposal—free prices applied logically, systematically, and courageously—can free us from the crony capitalist corruption and economic stagnation of the past, thereby opening up an economic future for everyone, not just the rich and powerful? Yes . Even the arch enemy of free prices, economist John Maynard Keynes, agreed that "ideas rule the world."[121]

It was not so long ago that humanity condemned economic competition and described economic change as evil. No wonder economic progress was unknown. Born poor, we died poor, with the limited exception of those few who controlled weapons and could take what they wanted, although under this system there was little to take. It was the gradual discovery of the power of free prices, beginning especially before the so-called industrial revolution, that allowed for the advancement of living standards even with population growth.

That revolution remains tragically unfinished today. Indeed it is in danger of being extinguished altogether by a resurgence of crony capitalism and controlled prices. But for our own sake, for the sake of the poor, and for the sake of our descendants, it is time to rediscover basic economic truth and re-commit to reform.

The founders of America laid it out: divide and thereby restrict government power. They explicitly told government to stay out of religion. They would have told government to stay out of the free price economic system if they had ever imagined it possible that public officials, financed and encouraged by special interests, would seize control of it. This was an oversight that can and should be corrected, preferably by Constitutional amendment. Let government pass laws that govern the economy and that apply to everyone with equal force. These laws will certainly set environmental and work standards as well as provide protection from violent force and fraud. But let there be no exceptions or special deals. Meanwhile let consumers, working through the market, control the economy through a system of free and unfettered prices.

Endnotes

1. *Forbes* (November 25, 1991): 128.

2. Alexander F. Skutch, *Moral Foundations* (Mt. Jackson, VA: Axios Press, 2007), 117-118.

3. Henry Hazlitt, *Economics in One Lesson* (New York: Harper & Brothers, 1946).

4. Lester Brown press release, November 6, 2001.

5. Anne Robert Jacques Turgot, *Eloge de Gournay* (1770); also in Denis Thomas, *The Mind of Economic Man* (Kent, UK: Quadrangle Books, 1970), 158.

6. John Maynard Keynes, BBC Broadcast (March 14, 1932), in *Collected Writings*, vol. 21, *Activities 1931–39: World Crisis and Policies in Britain and America* (London: Macmillan; New York: St. Martin's Press, 1982), 86, 92.

7. John Gunther, *Inside USA* (New York: Harper, 1946), 91.

8. Ludwig von Mises, *Human Action: A Treatise on Economics* (Chicago: Henry Regnery Company, 1966), 721.

9. Henry Hazlitt, *The Wisdom of Henry Hazlitt* (Irvington-Hudson: Foundation for Economic Education, 1993), 86.

10. Ted Honderich, *After the Terror* (Edinburgh: Edinburgh University Press, 2002), 137-38; cited in *Mises Review 9*, no.1 (Spring 2003): 15–16.

11. Karl Marx and Friedrich Engels, *The Communist Manifesto* (1848).

12. Howard Zinn, Emeritus Professor of History, Boston University and author of American history texts and other books, internet interview by David Barsamion, Boulder, CO, November 11, 1992.

13. Ludwig von Mises, *Economic Policy: Thoughts for Today and Tomorrow* (Lake Bluff, IL: Regnery Gateway, 1985), 3.

14. Milton Friedman, *Capitalism and Freedom* (Chicago: University of Chicago Press, 1962), 170.

15. Milton and Rose Friedman, *Free to Choose: A Personal Statement* (New York: Avon, 1981), 138.

16. Henry Hazlitt, *The Conquest of Poverty* (Irvington-on-Hudson, NY: Foundation for Economic Education, 1994), 51.

17. Mises, *Economic Policy*, 1.

18. Edwin Cannan, *An Economist's Protest* (New York: Adelphi Company, 1928), 429.

19. Mises, *Economic Policy,* 20.

20. Ibid.

21. A term coined by Michael Polanyi (1951); also see Sanford Ikeda, *Dynamics of the Mixed Economy: Toward a Theory of Interventionism* (London and New York: Routledge, 1997), 256 passim.

22. Walter Lippmann, *Interpretations: 1931–1932* (New York: Macmillan Company, 1932), 38.

23. Friedrich A. Hayek, "The Use of Knowledge in Society," *American Economic Review*, 35:4 (September 1945): 519–30. Reprinted in Friedrich A. Hayek, *Individualism and Economic Order* (Chicago: Henry Regnery Company, 1972), 77–91.

24. Adam Smith, *The Wealth of Nations*, bk. IV, chap. 2 (Edinburgh, 1776); also in G. Bannock, R. E. Baxter, and R. Reef, *The Penguin Dictionary of Economics* (London: Penguin Books, 1972), 247.

25. Wilhelm Röpke, *Economics of the Free Society* (Chicago: Henry Regnery Company, 1963), 235.

26. Marx and Engels, *The Communist Manifesto*.

27. Robert Skidelsky, *John Maynard Keynes*, vol. 2, *The Economist as Savior 1920–1937* (London: Macmillan, 2000), 233.

28. John Maynard Keynes, *The General Theory of Employment, Interest, and Money* (Amherst, NY: Prometheus Books, 1997), 372.

29. Norman Cott, *Free Market* (January 2003): 7.

30. *Forbes* (March 16, 1992): 64.

31. Arthur Okun, *Fortune* (November 1975): 199.

32. Friedman, *Free to Choose*, 137.

33. *Forbes* (August 6, 2001): 77.

34. P. T. Bauer, *Equality, the Third World, and Economic Delusion* (Cambridge, MA: Harvard University Press, 1981), 9.

35. Ibid., 10.

36. John Maynard Keynes, *Essays in Persuasion* (New York: W. W. Norton, 1963), 372.

37. Smith, *Wealth of Nations*, bk. 1, chap. 2, 20.

38. Ibid., bk. 4, 352.

39. *John Hussman Letter*, (December 3, 2012).

40. Adam Smith, *Lectures on Justice, Police, Revenue, and Arms*, 253–5; also in Cannan, *An Economist's Protest*, 425.

41. Adam Smith, *The Theory of Moral Sentiments*, (1759), 464–6; also in Cannan, *An Economist's Protest*, 425

42. George Stigler, *The Intellectual and the Market Place*, (Glencoe, IL: Free Press, 1963); also in Thomas, *Mind of Economic Man*, 148.

43. Geoffrey Martin Hodgson, *Economics and Utopia* (New York: Routledge, 1999), pt. III, 256; also in Charles Robert McCann, ed., *The Elgar Dictionary of Economic Quotations*, (Northampton, MA: Edward Elgar, 2003), 75

44. Letter to editor of Smith College campus newspaper, *Forbes* (July 21, 2003), 52.

45. Smith, *Wealth of Nations*, bk. IV, ch. 5.

46. http://www.mises.org/daily/6141 (August 23, 2012).

47. "From Yao to Mao," taped lecture.

48. Fernand Braudel, *Afterthoughts on Material Civilization and Capitalism* (Baltimore: John Hopkins University Press, 1977), 73.

49. Ibid., p. 74.

50. Sakudo, Management Practices, 150–51, 154; cited in David S. Landes, *The Wealth and Poverty of Nations: Why Some Are So Rich and Some Are So Poor* (New York: W. W. Norton, 1999), 362.

51. Landes, *The Wealth and Poverty of Nations*, 402.

52. Charles W. Cole, *French Mercantilism 1683–1700* (New York, 1943), 176; cited in Murray Rothbard, *Economic Thought Before Adam Smith: An Austrian Perspective on the History of Economic Thought*, vol. I (Cheltenham, UK: Edward Elgar, 1999), 219.

53. Keynes, *General Theory*, 351; also quoted in Henry Hazlitt, *The Failure of the "New Economics": An Analysis of the Keynesian Fallacies* (New Rochelle, NY: Arlington House, 1978), 184.

54. Keynes, *General Theory*, 164; and *Collected Writings* (vol. 21), 145.

55. Skidelsky, Oswald Falk Papers, in *John Maynard Keynes* (vol. 3), 21.

56. Rothbard, *Economic Thought Before Adam Smith*, 270.

57. John Hobson, *Richard Cobden: The International Man* (London: 1919), 392.

58. Entienne Bonnot, Abbé de Condillac, *Commerce and Government: Considered in their Mutual Relationship*, trans. Shelagh Eltis (Cheltenham, UK: Edward Elgar, 1997), 294.

59. Thomas Macaulay, *History of England* (1848), vol. 1, chap. 3; also quoted in Henry Hazlitt, *Economics in One Lesson* (San Francisco: Laissez Faire Books, 1996), 15.

60. *Weekly Standard* (March 14, 2005): 40.

61. Michael Grunwald, *Washington Post* (December 27, 2002): A-10.

62. Sanders, Sol, "What Obama Could Do," *Washington Times* (August 4, 2011).

63. Acemoglu et al, MIT, *The Value of Political Connections in the United States*, May 2009, revised December 2010.

64. http://www.bloomberg.com (October 27, 2009).

65. White House Meets Lobbyists Off Campus, http://www.politico.com (February 24, 2011), also *Washington Times* (July 5, 2010): 35.

66. Marc Thiessen, http://www.aei-ideas.org (September 15, 2012).

67. Choma, Russ, http://www.nbcnews.com (December 9, 2010).

68. Thomas, Evan (former editor of *Newsweek* then owned by *Post*), *Being Nixon* (New York, 2015), extract published online June 14, 2015.

69. See *New York Times* (July 20, 2004): A-22; "Evening Edition," NPR; and other sources.

70. Mises, *Economic Policy*, 52.

71. Novak, *Spirit of Democratic Capitalism*, 19–20.

72. Ibid., afterword.

73. http://www.realclearpolitics.com (September 2, 2010).

74. New Hampshire Democratic Party Convention, September 19, 2015.

75. Will, http://www.washingtonpost.com (January 5, 2012).

76. Paul Johnson, *History of Christianity* (New York: Simon and Schuster, 1976), Part 5.

77. The *Economist* (March 20, 2010): 91.

78. Caplan, http://www.econlong.econlib.org (March 4, 2010).

79. http://www.wsj.com (October 1, 2011).

80. Gunther, *Inside USA*, 918.

81. Ibid., 811.

82. Jim Rogers, Investment Biker, quoted on Roger's blog, accessed November 8, 2012.

83. House Ways and Means Committee, May 1939, quoted in Burton Folsom, *New Deal or Raw Deal? How FDR's Economic Legacy Has Damaged America* (New York: Threshold Editions, 2008); quoted Charen, http://www.nationalreview.com (November 25, 2012).

84. Lippmann, *The Good Society*, 119.

85. Conroy, http://www.realclearpolitics.com (December 6, 2012).

86. http://www.againstcronycapitalism.org (January 9, 2012).

87. Ibid. (July 16, 2012).

88. Thomas Sowell, http://www.townhall.com (December 12, 2012).

89. Alan Blinder, *Hard Heads, Soft Hearts: Tough-Minded Economics for a Just Society* (Cambridge, MA: Perseus Books, 1987); quoted in Samuelson, *Washington Post* (September 7, 1994): A21.

90. *Forbes* (August 6, 2001): 77.

91. Faber, *Gloom, Boom, and Doom Report* (May 14, 2011), 10.

92. Martin, Fridson, "Twisted Tariffs," *Barrons* (July 26, 2004).

93. M. Deane and R. Pringle, *The Central Banks* (London: Hamish Hamilton, 1994), n.p.; also in James Grant, *The Trouble with Prosperity: The Loss of Fear, the Rise of Speculation, and the Risk to American Savings* (New York: Times Books, 1996), 198.

94. Friedman, *Free to Choose*, 258.

95. Wanniski, *The Way the World Works*, 205.

96. *Business Week* (May 20, 1985): 38.

97. Jeff Madrick, *New York Review of Books* (May 3, 2001): 42.

98. Friedman, *Capitalism and Freedom*, 45.

99. James Grant, interview, *Austrian Economics Newsletter*, 16, no. 4 (Winter 1996): 2-3.

100. G. Epstein, interview, *Austrian Economics Newsletter*, 20 (2): 8.

101. *Grant's Interest Rate Observer* (July 13, 2012): 1.

102. Marc Faber, *Gloom, Boom, and Doom Report* (January 2013): 3.

103. *Harvard Magazine* (November-December 2008): 60.

104. *Grant's Interest Rate Observer* (April 3, 2015): 2.

105. Marc Faber, *Tomorrow's Gold: Asia's Age of Discovery* (Hong Kong: CLSA, 2002), 346–47.

106. "The Commanding Heights" (2002), Yergin, et al, a television documentary, PBS.

107. Rich Miller, *Bloomberg News* (May 19, 2009).

108. George Akerlof and Robert Shiller, *Animal Spirits* (Princeton, NJ: Princeton University Press, 2009); see also Benjamin Friedman for a review of Akerlof and Shiller, *New York Review* (May 28, 2009): 44. In his review, Friedman notes that he made a similar proposal in "Monetary Policy with a Credit Aggregate Target," *Journal of Monetary Economics* (Spring 1983 Supplement).

109. http://www.againstcronycapitalism.org (November 28, 2011).

110. *Forbes* (July 16, 2012): 24.

111. Lawrence Kotlikoff, http://www.bloomberg.com (September 28, 2011).

112. Ken Mayland, http://www.marketwatch.com (August 16, 2010).

113. Ayres and Edlin, *New York Times* (December 19, 2011): A-29.

114. Quoted in *Grant's Interest Rate Observer* (June 15, 2012): 5.

115 William Pesek, http://www.bloomberg.com (May 21, 2012).

116. http://www.againstcronycapitalism.org (June 8, 2012).

117. *Grant's Interest Rate Observer* (July 13, 2012): 1.

118. Pipes, http://www.forbes.com (August 20, 2012).

119. Smith, http://www.nypost.com (October 2, 2010).

120. *Weekly Standard* (January 19, 2009): 20.

121. See end of Keynes's, *General Theory*.

One Hundred
Economic Laws

Preface

THE CONCEPT OF economic law was once a familiar feature of everyone's education. It was taken for granted that they existed. The difficulty was discovering what they were and elucidating them for the enlightenment and betterment of humanity. They were also assumed to be complex, so that after economists worked them out through abstruse investigations and debates, they would have to be translated for lay people.

In more recent years, another idea has gained ground: that while physical laws certainly do exist and help us manage our lives better, economic laws do not really exist or at least have no predictive value whatsoever. This thesis has been argued in a 2013 *Atlantic* article by an expert titled "The 'Laws of Economics' Don't Exist."

This *Atlantic* article assumes that economic laws must be derived from massive amounts of data, without explaining why this must be so, and claims that we simply lack enough systematic economic history to draw any conclusions. This is wrong for reasons that will shortly be explained.

The author also writes that "I may agree that the war on drugs is flawed, but not because it violates 'laws of economics,' . . . rather because it fails in most of its basic goals." This is actually contradictory. Laws of economics are based on our own human logic. A public policy or private action that is inconsistent with its most basic goals violates logic, and by doing so, violates economic law as well.

Lawrence Summers, former Treasury Secretary under President Clinton, President of Harvard, and Chief Economic Advisor to President Obama, evidently does believe that economic laws exist. He wrote an article in the *Washington Post* shortly after President Trump's election titled "Trump Can't Repeal the Laws of Economics." Summers did not, however, give any specific examples of the laws of economics he had in mind.

The ideas that have been organized and presented in this book under the term "economic law" have been developed (and frequently corrected) by numerous economists over the centuries. The most notable contribution by far was made by the twentieth-century economist Ludwig von Mises, although it should be emphasized that he did not present his own ideas as a system of laws, but rather as a treatise that often made reference to underlying laws.

At the onset of Mises's masterpiece, *Human Action*, we have this discussion of how the discovery of the concept of economic law changed human history:

> The discovery of the inescapable interdependence of market phenomena . . . [produced] a new view of society. . . . Bewildered . . . [at first], people . . . learned . . . that there is another aspect . . . [of] human action . . . than that of good and bad, of fair and unfair, of just and unjust. In the course of social events, there prevails a regularity of phenomena to which man must adjust his action if he wishes to succeed. . . . [Despite their differences], one must study the laws of human action and social cooperation as the physicist studies the laws of nature. Human action and social cooperation seen as the object of a science of given relations, no longer as a normative discipline of things that ought to be—this was a revolution of tremendous consequences for knowledge and philosophy as well as for social action.[1]

Mises's students Friedrich Hayek and Murray Rothbard also contributed many insights about economic law. Another contemporary and friend, Henry Hazlitt, in turn described many of these same ideas with unparalleled clarity in both books and articles.

In some cases, the names of economic laws were developed long ago, and are now settled. No one would ever call the law of supply and demand anything else, although they might call it the principle of supply and demand or just "supply and demand."

The law of marginal utility may sound needlessly obscure or jargonish, but has too much history even to think of rephrasing it. As groundbreaking as the law of marginal utility was (and is), it is presented in this book not as a standalone law, but as a corollary (derivative) of another law. The logic behind the laws is often highly interrelated, so the order of presentation matters. In this book, there are twenty principal laws and eighty corollaries, each of which could be considered a law in its own right, which is why the title is *One Hundred Economic Laws*.

Although for some economic laws (e.g. supply and demand and marginal utility) there is a well-established terminology, in other instances, there is not. The goal in developing terminology for this book has been to keep it clear and free of technical language. The reader should feel free to substitute his or her own terms and descriptions, to challenge whether some of the laws really qualify as laws, and to identify laws that should be added to the list.

Economics is a collaborative and cumulative discipline. This can lead to serious lapses in logic, self-deception, or, worse, deliberate deception. Self-deception may be closely linked to deliberate deception if someone's personal income, career standing, and prestige depend on promoting untruths, and both forms of deception are particularly acute in economics.

Over the years, no other scientific discipline has been so plagued by "thinkers for hire" lavishly rewarded by special economic interests. But it must be acknowledged that this practice is increasingly spreading within the physical sciences as well, because of the high financial and political stakes in industries closely connected to government, including, among others, drugs, biotechnology, chemicals, energy, and farming.

Even so, there is no place for dismissal, disdain, or mockery in economics. We owe each other a respectful hearing, if only because, being human, we are prone to logical errors, and can learn from listening.

We will now attempt to establish, as briefly as possible, what economic laws are, what they tell us about economic life, and how we can use them to guide our actions and choices in an uncertain world.

It is hoped that most readers will start with the first law and proceed from there through the hundredth. Each law builds a further foundation for what follows. Alternatively, there is a summary list of the one hundred laws at the back of the book without explanation or commentary, but noting the page where explanation or commentary may be found. In this way, readers who wish to browse can pick out particular laws they wish to read about.

Chapter I

Laws of Economic Analysis

1. *Law of Analytic Laws*: If . . . then analysis assists us just as much in the social realm as in the physical realm.

AN ANALYTIC LAW is a definable, regular, and predictable feature of physical or social reality. Physical reality: if we touch a hot stove top, we may burn our finger. Social reality: if we walk into a war zone, we may be killed.

Studying analytic law and applying what we learn helps us meet our objectives, whatever they are. Conversely, we ignore such knowable features of reality at our peril. All such laws are self-enforcing. We submit to them or we face a penalty, not every time perhaps, but often. We may injure ourselves. We may fail at what we hope to do. We may even, as in the above example, die.

Whether they describe the physical or the social world, analytic laws should not be confused with manmade laws. If we take the risk of walking into a war zone or even a crime-ridden urban area, we are not usually violating any manmade law. We are rather taking a risk with a knowable analytic law of social life.

2. *Corollary A of Law of Analytic Laws: Material Life* (If we restrict our inquiry to material life, we will misunderstand economic laws.)

Although a subset of social life, economic action is not just about the material side of our existence. It expresses our mind. Our mind is just as important as our bodies in defining our material wants and goals.

People act. They act purposefully. They have reasons. Their actions reflect beliefs, values, and preferences as well as physical needs. Diners at a restaurant do not just rate the food. They rate the presentation. They may appreciate something as intangible as candle light. We may also appreciate the meal more if we have worked hard to earn the money to pay for it.

There is no such being as *homo economicus*, the hyper-rationalist straw man found in some economic theories and textbooks. There are only complete human beings interacting socially. For any economic law to be valid, it must apply to people as they are and social life as it is.

3. *Corollary B of Law of Analytic Laws: Boundaries* (If we look for economic laws only outside ourselves, we will also misunderstand them.)

The physical world is both inside and outside ourselves. So is the social world. We maintain a constant dialogue within ourselves in addition to our dialogue with others. Therefore economic laws, to be valid, must apply to all our social reality, both internal and external. We even make deals and exchanges with ourselves: I may decide I can have dessert, but only if I exercise.

4. *Corollary C of Law of Analytic Laws: Physical Science Myopia* (If we only look through the lens of the physical sciences, we will also misunderstand economic and other social laws.)

Experimental science and economics both generate laws. In both cases, we utilize all our mental tools (emotional, intuitive, empirical, and logical) to identify the laws and the latter two especially to communicate them to others. But the process is very different.

We cannot generate economic laws through controlled experiments, as we try to do in the physical sciences. Controlled experiments do not exist in the social realm and would not be helpful even if they could exist.

Watching an apple fall from a tree does not change the trajectory of the apple. But learning about ourselves can significantly change our trajectory. The social and economic realm is comprised of human choices and those choices are always changing. Just hearing someone expound an economic law may itself change our choices and actions and thus our economic reality.

In some cases, we think we have discerned an economic law only to discover that it is a falsehood. If everyone becomes convinced that stocks are a better investment than bonds, everyone will buy stocks, their prices will soar unsustainably followed by a crash, and then nobody will want stocks. This has happened many times in economic history.

There is an argument for the superiority of stocks over bonds, but it is not a law, and we cannot rely on it to guide our day-to-day choices. The reasoning involved becomes more reliable if it includes consideration of the price at which we buy the stock, but this cannot be formulated as a law, either.

It is an economic law to state that buying a stock without regard for price will increase the probabilities of incurring a loss, but this is not a particularly useful economic law. It is not particularly useful because, like many economic laws, it is so entirely self-evident that we already know it, although at times our emotions may carry us away and a reminder may still be useful.

The most important and helpful economic laws are those that accurately describe social reality, that may require some careful reflection, but that on reflection are self-evident, and that provide meaningful guidance as we go about making our choices. In this book, we will try to focus on some of these more important economic laws. Readers will inevitably have different views about the extent to which they meet all these criteria.

5. Corollary D of Law of Analytic Laws: Logic (If we concentrate on ordinary logic, the kind of logic we use to police our everyday language, it will give us the best results in identifying, defining, and using economic laws.)

As noted above, we all rely in part on our empirical brains (utilizing observation, experience, even history) in deciding how to operate socially. But our interpretations of experience and especially second-hand experience in the form of history are too diverse to allow consensus. Whatever seems self-evident to you about the historical record will likely not be self-evident to others. Ordinary logic is much more useful in trying to separate fact from fiction and communicating that fact to others.

For a statement to be logical, it must be clear, organized, orderly, relevant, complete, and consistent. Of these tests, inconsistency is the easiest to spot and therefore the most immediately useful.

This kind of logic is not an abstract exercise unrelated to the facts of our actual life. On the contrary, it helps us stay connected to reality, to avoid the human temptation to confuse our wishes with the real world. Nor is it very complicated.

It is not necessary to set pencil to paper in order to demonstrate the impossibility of constructing a triangular square. We do not need experience to confirm what is already self-evident: we are contradicting ourselves. Most economic laws are of this nature. Their purpose is to keep our thoughts and actions from being either internally contradictory or inconsistent with the reality of the external world.

A square by definition must have four equal sides. The idea of a triangle cannot be made consistent with it. Similarly, economic laws should be logically self-evident, that is, implicit or at least implied in their own terms. Conversely, the reverse of these laws should be contradictory by their own terms.

As economist Ludwig von Mises explained:

> The idea that A could at the same time be non-A or that to prefer A to B could at the same time be to prefer B to A is simply inconceivable and absurd to a human mind.[2] . . . [This kind of logical] . . . reasoning is . . . deductive. It cannot produce anything else but . . . analytic judgments. All its implications are logically derived from the premises

and were already contained in them.... The significant task of [this] ... reasoning is on the one hand to bring into relief all that is implied in the categories, concepts, and premises and, on the other hand, to show what they do not imply.[3]

It is vain to object that life and reality are not logical. Life and reality are neither logical nor illogical; they are simply given. But logic is the only tool available to man for the comprehension of both.... As far as man is able to attain any knowledge, however limited, he can use only one avenue of approach, that opened by reason....[4]

The very existence of human reason is a nonrational fact. The only statement that can be predicated with regard to reason is that it is the mark that distinguishes man from animals and has brought about everything that is specifically human....[5]

If logic is shared by all humanity, so are logical lapses. Because we have the power to choose, we may even consciously choose illogic, although, when we do, we cannot entirely escape inconvenient messages from the logical side of our brain.

All of us, very much including economists, are illogical in different ways and from different motives. We may not be careful in our language, which leads to false conclusions, or we fail to take the time to grasp the full implications of a statement, or we may intentionally use language to confuse or mislead rather than to clarify and instruct (sometimes called "spin") or, worse, we may lie outright to protect some material interest. Economic debates are especially beset with such problems, because very large sums of money may be at stake.

Who can forget President George W. Bush saying on national television during the Crash of 2008: "I've abandoned free market principles to save the free market system."[6] Perhaps he had heard this oxymoronic claim from his treasury secretary, the former CEO of Goldman Sachs, who at that moment was working to save his former firm, and, it might be added, his stock holdings in it, from his powerful post within the government. Perhaps the president had heard it from a White House economist. In either case, the advisor had probably not meant for this bit of sophistry to be repeated in public.

Eighteenth-century philosopher and economist David Hume long ago warned of these same pitfalls:

> It must be owned, that nothing can be of more use than to improve, by practice, the method of reasoning on ... [economic topics], which of all others are the most important, though they are commonly treated in the loosest and most careless manner.[7]

6. *Corollary E of Law of Analytic Laws: Mathematics* (It is an essential tool for economic calculation, but if we try to use it in the same way it is used in the physical sciences, the results will not be helpful to us.)

Both experimental science and economics utilize math of one kind or another. But it is not the same math. Economics relies heavily on arithmetic because economic calculation (the definition of assets, liabilities, income, expenses, and profit) requires it. In addition, ordinal numbers (first, second, etc.) help us define and communicate important priorities and preferences. On the other hand, as economist Ludwig von Mises emphasized, attempts to utilize higher math for purposes beyond economic description or illustration have generally led to unrealistic and contradictory end results.

This has been and continues to be difficult for economists to accept. Because economic law is primarily derived by a process of logic, because all math is a tool of logic, and because higher math plays such an important role in the physical sciences, many incorrectly infer that higher math should play a major role in developing and defining economic law. The reality is that we can succeed in capturing the underlying logic of human action and detecting contradictory action by analyzing the speech we use to describe the action. No matter how hard we try, we can never capture human action in equations, if only because human action is so interactive and changeable.

Given that the very purpose of laws is to enable us to recognize and adapt ourselves to reality, make better choices, and thus help us realize our social and economic objectives, economists should reconsider their current reliance on algebra, trigonometry, calculus, and related quantitative modeling techniques, none of which have produced reliable guidance for our economic choices.

7. **Corollary F of Law of Analytic Laws: Economic Data (Observations from the past are not relevant or reliable enough for more than limited use. If you base decisions on old correlations, you will likely make poor decisions.)**

Economics is full of laws claiming to show a constant relationship between some recorded series, such as the price of two commodities, because there has been a noticeable and seemingly measurable relationship in the past. Causality is then inferred from correlation (A not only happened with B, but it also was caused by B). Unfortunately, even the correlations, much less the inferences of causation, are necessarily spurious. They also contradict the reality of constant change in human choice.

Famous economist Milton Friedman thought he saw a powerful correlation between levels of consumer prices and some particular preceding money supply measurements. Eureka. All that had to be done to control prices was to control those money supply series. Not surprisingly, it did not work out.

Money is difficult to define (most of the standard government definitions are flawed), much less measure. Although the amount of money is critical for prices, what ultimately controls them is what people expect to happen to them.

Historic episodes of consumer price inflation, such as the German inflation following World War I, have been triggered by too much money being created by government. But eventually prices begin to rise faster than the money creation, because the price rise is driven by people's fear of the money creation as much as by the money creation itself.

In real life, people act, they change their minds, they influence each other, what Freidman and other economists say about the process also influences them. This cannot be measured on a graph. Even if it appears measurable, beware drawing any conclusion from it.

Sometimes the data being studied, graphed, and relied upon is so airy and immaterial that it can hardly even be called data. Federal Reserve Governor Lael Brainard gave a speech in 2016 in which she indicated the Fed was watching changes in a survey of consumer inflation expectations conducted by the University of Michigan. Jim Grant of *Grant's Interest Rate Observer* sardonically noted that:

> Random people, asked to guess where the CPI [consumer price index] might be trending in . . . [that year or five years later] did

> not [honestly] reply, "I don't even know
> where it is now. . . . Respondents rather
> vouchsafed an answer . . . [which] was . . .
> [a quarter of one percent] lower than the
> guesses previously submitted by previous
> random people since 2006."[8]

The "data dependent" Fed supposedly relied at least in part on this "data" in choosing not to increase interest rates.

Even less logical are graphs and would-be laws trying to show a relationship between physical and economic series. For example, the distinguished nineteenth-century economist William Stanley Jevons, whom we will mention again when we get to the important economic idea of marginal utility, thought he had found a regularity between business cycles and sunspot cycles. He attributed this to some kind of agricultural influence, at a time when agriculture was by far the largest human industry. Scientists subsequently corrected their sunspot data calculations, which destroyed the reported relationship. As this illustrates, it is easy for human beings, including economists, to operate in a fog of supposed facts and to draw completely erroneous conclusions from them.

8. *Corollary G of Law of Analytic Laws: Predicting the Future* (In relying on economic laws, we should understand that they are usually probabilistic in nature.)

The physical sciences have gained their present immense prestige in part because they can be used to predict the future. Even this achievement must be qualified. If we drop a piece of paper from a tall building, the law of gravity will ensure that it eventually hits the ground, but we will not know where or when. Science cannot reliably predict constantly changing conditions such as wind and weather, although it may be able to give us probabilities, and it can precisely predict how much wind pressure a structure will be able to withstand, given some further assumptions, such as the quality of construction materials.

Social reality is constantly changing. Although the term is often used (or rather misused) by economists, there is no such thing as social or economic equilibrium. None of our decisions as human beings are fixed, all are to some degree forever in flux. And there are billions of us, all interacting to some degree with each other, and nothing about our relations is truly fixed, either. In economics, there are few certainties, mostly probabilities, and even the probabilities do not lend themselves to standard mathematical treatment.

If we are a baker, we may think we know what wheat costs, but the mere possibility of some new drought or some new aversion to eating gluten may change the price overnight. Just as in the physical sciences, but perhaps even more so, the probabilities will tend to be vague about the timing of how events may unfold. No matter how certain we are that actions taken in violation of economic law will come to no good end, the timing will remain uncertain, and the same is true for actions taken with better odds for success, however we have defined success.

Life requires a great deal of persistence and patience, and so does economics. But if we are patient, and if we want to improve our conditions, economic law shows us the way forward out of poverty and into wealth. Given sufficient time, the wealth creation can be staggering. We will have more to say about this in later sections.

9. *Corollary H of Law of Analytic Laws: Immutability* (No matter how much we change, the underlying tenets of economic law do not change.)

As we have discussed, the law of gravity is not tangibly affected by our observation of it, although the statement has been somewhat qualified by quantum physics. By contrast, our own behavior is directly affected by our observation of it. Does this mean that economic laws are changeable, that what was once true may now be false, that such laws continually arise and pass away, that we must continually search for new ones? No.

At least the underlying tenets of economic laws never change, no matter how much we change, because they are based on the underlying logic of our social realities, including our own nature. This logic is both fixed and inescapable. To take the simplest example, you cannot expect friendship from others without offering friendship in return. This will never change, so long as we exist in our human form. A law or corollary of a law related to central banking might have to be modified if central banks disappear, but the underlying theme of the law will remain intact and forever relevant.

10. *Corollary I of Law of Analytic Laws: Universality* (Economic laws apply without exception to everyone.)

Economic law does not speak in a religious or moral voice, although by reminding us of the inescapable realities we must face in life, it may influence, even heavily influence, our choices in these and all other spheres. Its general methodology is to advise us that if our goal is A (for example less poverty and more prosperity), then approach B is more likely to help us realize it over time with fewer negative effects than approach C or D. This applies to anyone, whatever their personal goals may be.

11. *Corollary J of Law of Analytic Laws: Corruption* (If we rely on laws, physical or social, there will be attempts to corrupt and misuse them.)

Experimental science (together with its chief tool experimental method) and economic law (together with its chief tool economic calculation) are arguably the greatest achievements of modern civilization, although the latter is too often taken for granted or denigrated. Both are constructions of the human mind and are therefore vulnerable to the dishonesty and corruption that plague human life. As previously mentioned, laboratory scientists may cheat on their results or sell out to special interests in exchange for grants. Economists may be more interested in power, wealth, or just an easier life than in seeking out or sharing the truth. This is a reality, too.

In other instances, it is not the experts, but ordinary people who may hammer away at the foundations of experimental science or economic law precisely because they find these disciplines inconvenient. For example, in 2016 students at Cape Town University staged a protest claiming that science is inherently racist, which by definition it cannot be, if it is truly science. The students call themselves "fallists" with a hashtag of "Science Must Fall." This does not appear to be merely adolescent fun, but rather a genuine failure to grasp that the law of gravity has no logical connection to social justice.[9]

Chapter 11

Laws of Economic Sustainability

12. *Law of Sustainability*: Economic laws are concerned with and also help guide us toward sustainability.

THIS COULD ALSO be called Henry Hazlitt's Law, Laozi's Law, Epicurus's Law, or Aristotle's Law, in that elements of it have been expressed by each of them. Every action that we take will have near-term and longer-term consequences. It will also have consequences that are visible or readily foreseeable along with consequences that are difficult or sometimes impossible to discern or foresee.

Moreover, every change that we seek or achieve will have at least some negative as well as positive elements.

And every virtue taken to an extreme may become a vice. We know all this, but we too often try to ignore it. Public officials are especially prone to forget or ignore it.

Because it is natural human behavior to focus on the near term and on what can readily be seen, to consider one factor to the exclusion of others, and to take things to an extreme, economic law focuses on the opposite. Its central theme is sustainability. It helps guide us toward actions that have a greater potential to be sustainable.

13. *Corollary A of Law of Sustainability: Unintended Consequences* (A refusal to think sustainably produces unintended negative consequences. In some cases, these are readily foreseeable, in other cases not.)

A useful illustration is libertarian Richard Cowan's Iron Law of Prohibition (1986). Speaking of the prohibition of liquor sales in the US in the 1920s and the later war on drugs, Cowan wrote that "The harder the enforcement, the harder the drugs."[10]

Economist Mark Thornton agrees and offers further illustrations. Beer and wine drinkers switched to the hardest liquor during and after Prohibition, drank more, and continued this habit for the rest of their lives. The five martini business lunch, common in the 1950s and 1960s, was directly traceable to a government policy that ended in the early 1930s.

Marijuana sold on the street became increasingly potent because it was easier and more profitable to transport and sell in small amounts. For a similar reason, bulky opium became concentrated heroin, and cocaine became crack cocaine.[11]

Smoking cigarettes is not illegal, but government taxes have been piled so high that it has spawned a national and international trade in cigarette smuggling. There are reports that terrorist organizations have gotten involved. A global cigarette smuggling ring was even discovered within the Iraqi mission to the United Nations. It made profits of millions of dollars using diplomatic pouches to move its goods.[12] How long will it be before smugglers start making their own cigarettes and concentrating toxic as well as unknown ingredients in them?

Note that all these consequences were unintended, but not unforeseeable. If we take the time and trouble to think through our proposed actions, as economic analysis requires, we can foresee many, if not necessarily all, of the secondary or distant effects.

Further along, when we come to discuss laws of prices and money, we will see that the law of unintended consequences also helps explain why government attempts to stabilize prices and the economy as a whole are necessarily destabilizing.

Chapter III

Laws of the Division of Labor

14. *Law of the Division of Labor*: If we share labor, we may be able to make ourselves much more productive.

THIS MAY SOUND obvious, but we have to think through all the implications. Adam Smith took pains to illustrate some of the advantages of a division of labor by describing a pin factory in the beginning of his famous 1776 book *Wealth of Nations*. There is a very complex division of labor within our own bodies. There is also division of labor within ant and bee colonies and within wolf packs.

Human societies are unique in many ways, not least in that we kill our own kind. If we do not treat others

as enemies, seek to kill them, and seize their possessions, we have to choose a method of co-existing, or
even better, of cooperating to our mutual advantage.

15. *Corollary A of Law of the Division of Labor: Voluntary Exchange* (If we emphasize not just exchange of labor, but voluntary exchange of both labor and goods, we will get better and more reliable results.)

There are only two major methods to elicit the kind
of cooperation needed to divide productive labor
and enter into exchanges: force or incentive. For an
exchange to be driven by incentive, it must be voluntary. The exchange need not be material. We may
exchange friendship for friendship, which then leads
to and supports many other exchanges.

The concept of voluntary exchange is a natural part
of our psyche. Most modern European languages are
believed to descend from a common Indo-European
root, and in that early language, a single word seems
to have sufficed for both giving and receiving. In early
man's mind, the two acts were so closely related that
one word sufficed.

Voluntary exchange is logically much more effective
and productive than the use of force. The latter not
only requires an enormous expenditure of resources,
energy, and time to maintain discipline. In addition,
it creates both active and passive resistance. Human

beings are very good at passive resistance, especially over long periods of time, which can eventually sap even the best-organized enterprises. Terror can be used against passive resistance, as Stalin and Mao showed, but it is very difficult to sustain. Quite apart from moral considerations, voluntary exchange is potentially much more productive.

16. *Corollary B of Law of the Division of Labor: Private Ownership* (If we are to exchange, we must first own.)

In the first place, we must own our own labor and not be enslaved by other people or by government. Note that private and government bondage are closely linked. Slavery in any form represents the ultimate form of market monopoly, and, like other monopolies, cannot survive without government enforcement.

Beyond our own labor, we must also have ownership of our possessions, if we are to trade them for other possessions. The chief threat to our ownership is fraud, theft, and violence, all of which are supposed to be barred by an effectively functioning government. But for much of human history, it has been impossible to bring possessions out into the light of day to trade or use for investment purposes, because government itself was likely to steal them.

17. *Corollary C of Law of the Division of Labor: (Law of) Potential Diseconomies of Scale* (If we exchange labor, it must be carefully organized, or we may become less, not more productive.)

Any voluntary and cooperative division of labor must overcome natural constraints. Assume that one craftsman builds an automobile from scratch in his own workshop. Now assume that a hundred such craftsman are assembled and invited to work together.

At first, chaos results and fewer automobiles are produced. But, given time, the craftsmen figure out how to divide the labor and also how to take further advantage of the division of labor by introducing shared mechanization. They become more productive than before, and this is confirmed by the production of a larger number of automobiles each year with the same amount of inputs or the same number with fewer inputs.

18. *Corollary D of Law of the Division of Labor: (Law of) Diminishing Returns* (If we add to one input without considering the effect on other inputs and the total process, we may disrupt rather than enhance production.)

Given the state of current knowledge, technology, and capital, there is an optimum amount of inputs for any production process. If we fail to pay close attention to this fact, we will fail. At the very least, we will create needless waste.

For example, if we are using one ton of steel to make the automobiles in the prior example, and this is indeed optimum, ordering two tons of steel per vehicle will just cause waste, unnecessary cost, and confusion for the shop. Two tons per car cannot pay unless there is a fundamental reworking of the product or its production process.

Corollary D is really just a variant way of stating the risks expressed in Corollary C. In C, the focus is on the importance of organizing labor to improve productivity. In D, the focus is on understanding and organizing other factor inputs effectively.

A variant of this law, sometimes called Liebig's Law of the Minimum, states that in some cases what seems a small element of the production process can prove to be so scarce, hard to obtain, or hard to obtain in quantity at a reasonable price that it completely frustrates efforts to scale up. There have been concerns that sourcing rare earth minerals might at some point represent this kind of a problem for high-tech products, especially high-tech weapons.

19. *Corollary E of Law of the Division of Labor: (Law of) Potential Economies of Scale* (If we scale up in a logical way, it can make us far more productive.)

This is the obverse of corollaries B and C. It has major real world consequences. Organized properly, larger scale production can be much more effective and efficient. It can either produce more goods or the same number of goods at a lower cost or both.

Potential economies of scale from larger-scale production may be measurable after the fact but are not measurably predictable. They require both effective management and larger-scale markets to buy the production. There are always many barriers, particularly political barriers, to the creation and maintenance of large-scale markets, some of which may be difficult to foresee.

20. Corollary F of Law of the Division of Labor: (Law of) Comparative Advantage, also called Law of Shared Advantage (Even if different parties or countries are ill-matched in skill or resources, they will do better cooperating.)

As noted above, an effectively organized division of labor offers the potential to become ever more productive as the scale of cooperation increases. In the automobile example above, all the craftsmen were equally skilled. Even so, they had to organize themselves differently in order to take advantage of economies of scale.

What happens when the producers are not equally skilled at everything, when some are more skilled at one thing, while others are more skilled at another? In this case, cooperation could be even more beneficial, because dividing up the tasks will be easier. Each person (or country) can concentrate on what it does best while relying on co-workers to accomplish other essential tasks.

21. *Corollary G of Law of the Division of Labor: (Law of) Absolute Advantage* **(Even if one party or country has all the skills and resources and the other has none, they are still better off cooperating.)**

Even in this extreme case, in which one party or country has an absolute advantage in everything, the law of absolute advantage demonstrates that they are better off cooperating. For example, imagine an engineer with his own consulting firm and an unskilled laborer who needs work. Although the engineer might be more skilled at everything that takes place in the firm to start, even at sorting or sending out mail or cleaning the office, he or she is better off to hire the unskilled laborer, first to clean the office, then to take over clerical tasks, and eventually perhaps to handle clients and other more demanding tasks.

The same observation holds true for different countries. One country can hypothetically be more efficient than the other in making all products (i.e. possesses an absolute advantage in its resources and skill set). But the skilled country is better off concentrating on those areas in which it has the relatively greatest advantage and buying imports of products in which its advantage is less pronounced.

The doctrines of comparative and absolute advantage were developed most thoroughly by early 19th century English economist David Ricardo, but contemporary American economist Thomas Sowell provides a good example of the latter in his book *Basic Economics*. He asks us to assume, for purpose of illustration, that the United States makes both shirts and shoes more cheaply than Canada. In other words, the US has an absolute advantage in both articles. Specifically, the US makes shirts more than twice as cheaply and shoes 25% more cheaply.

Since the US is much more cost-effective in shirts, relatively speaking, than it is in shoes, it will still pay to concentrate on shirts and leave the shoes to Canada. If the US and Canada team up in this way, the total production of shirts and shoes mathematically increases by about 20% and 11%, respectively. Just by specializing and trading, the two countries in this example become measurably richer.[13] This is of course a hypothetical example, because in real life many factors can destroy the opportunities created by dividing up production tasks across ever-widening markets.

One of the factors that tend to thwart full utilization of the laws of comparative and absolute advantage is our ignorance of their benefits. As eighteenth-century philosopher and economist David Hume pointed out:

> Nothing is more usual, among states which
> have made some advances in commerce,

than to look on the progress of their neighbors with a suspicious eye, to consider all trading states as their rivals, and to suppose that it is impossible for any of them to flourish, but at their expense. In opposition to this narrow and malignant opinion, I will venture to assert, that the increase of riches and commerce in any one nation, instead of hurting, commonly promotes the riches and commerce of all its neighbors; and that a state can scarcely carry its trade and industry very far, where all the surrounding states are buried in ignorance, sloth, and barbarism. . . .[14]

22. Corollary H of Law of the Division of Labor: Deceptive Trade Practices (What is called "free trade" by governments may actually be the opposite of genuine free trade and may destroy the potential benefits of a global division of labor.)

Another barrier to the full utilization of the laws of comparative and absolute advantage is the tendency of governments to allow special interests to write trade laws and treaties. Because these laws and treaties matter so much to corporate interests in particular, this practice can yield a rich harvest of campaign contributions and other assistance, and it can all be done under the cover of economic nationalism. As a result, what are usually described by governments as "free trade" deals with other countries may actually be better described as crony trade deals.

The situation becomes even more complex when a country such as the US has a "reserve" currency, which means that it can borrow abroad but still be able to repay in dollars. Other non-reserve countries borrow abroad at considerable risk, because if they borrow in another currency and the price of their own currency plummets, the amount to be repaid soars. By contrast, the US since World War II has been in a position where it can repay its foreign loans just by printing more dollars. Not surprisingly, under these circumstances, it has imported vastly more than it has exported and covered the difference by borrowing. Such a situation is inherently unstable and leads to all sorts of economic posturing and games. American economist Merton Miller has explained the situation this way:

> We've actually been playing a cruel trick on the Japanese [and Chinese]. We've persuaded them to send us expensive [goods]—and in exchange we give them pictures of George Washington.... [If] they want ... their money ... , "Okay," we say, ... "[but if you try to sell the US currency that we give you on world markets, you may only get] 20 cents on the dollar." They're the losers at this game.[15]

Economist Paul McCulley agrees:

> To those with Calvinistic tendencies, always
> looking for what can go wrong, . . . the no-
> tion of . . . [the United States financing its
> consumption by borrowing from China]
> just doesn't seem right. . . . But . . . [at least
> for the moment] it is good, very good.[16]

All this may sound good to Miller and McCulley, but
it is a perversion of the law of comparative and absolute advantage and therefore will inevitably prove to be
unsustainable. When this finally becomes apparent, it
will, once again, be the poor and the middle class who
pay the heaviest price.

23. *Corollary I of Law of the Division of Labor: Scale of Participation* (If people choose not to participate in shared labor, either because they do not work at all or because they do not share their work, everyone will have less than they might have had.)

Degree of participation matters. Many people will not
be able to participate in the sharing of labor because
they cannot labor. They may be too young, too old, or
disabled. If people not in these categories choose not
to participate, but still share in the fruits of labor, then
incentives for those participating will be reduced,
because there will be less to share.

Chapter IV

Laws of Prices

24. *Law of Prices*: If we wish to cooperate on a voluntary basis, we must have shared, workable, flexible prices.

AN ECONOMIC SYSTEM based on a division of labor and mutual exchange cannot function without workable market prices. In today's world, we depend on these prices for our very survival. If they disappeared suddenly, and we had to fall back on barter, there would be absolute chaos, followed quickly by shortages. Most of us would starve.

Prices allow us to exchange goods and services in ever widening circles. If we live on a self-sufficient manor, as in Middle Age Europe, we do not need prices to make exchanges. One farmer on a rare occasion trades four sheep for a cow while another trades at a different ratio according to his needs and preferences, but no one else need pay much attention.

It is quite different exchanging at a distance. In this case, we need not only to know what the expected price is at the moment. We also need some assurance that we will receive payment. This is much more complicated.

A worldwide system of prices enormously simplifies economic life. It tells producers what to produce, how to produce it, and in what amount. It does not reveal everything. Prices alone do not tell us why the cost of bread is rising or falling. But by weighing, balancing, and anticipating supply and demand, they provide enough information to make rational economic decisions.

In order to play this weighing and balancing role, they must be flexible, free to move either up or down, and this applies to wages as well as other prices.

25. *Corollary A of Law of Prices: (Law of) Discovery and Communication* (If shared prices are to help us, they must operate as both a discovery and information system.)

Economist Friedrich Hayek observed that market prices constitute a "discovery system."[17] They not only discover what is scarce, what is available. They also communicate it efficiently. This is only possible when market prices are allowed to discover who has what, who wants what, what might change, and what prices will bring seller and buyer into a voluntary and mutually beneficial exchange. It is unarguable that prices manipulated or tightly controlled by government authorities cannot help us "discover" or communicate any of this.

26. Corollary B of Law of Prices: (Law of) Order (If we allow prices to do their job, they will create, maintain, and enhance economic and social order.)

The term "spontaneous order" was coined by economist Michael Polanyi. We see this phenomenon both in nature and in social life. We do not consciously order our lungs to breathe, but breathe they do, for as long as a century. Everything in our body interrelates and interacts to keep us alive without any central direction. Language provides a prime example from the social realm. No authority other than the French Academy has ever tried to control it, the Academy largely failed, yet French and other languages remain as serviceable as ever. Common law operates in a similar way. It provides precedents without anyone deliberately trying to guide or control it.

Consider what a miracle it is to be able to read a book. Whether it is delivered on paper that is derived from wood or electronically, millions of people, each with a distinct expertise, must work together to make it happen. No government planner oversees the process. No group of government planners would ever have the necessary expertise to know how to assemble all the parts, stationary and moving, required to make a product as simple as a pencil, nor would they be able to coordinate all the necessary actions.

The key word is action. It is sometimes said that an economy is like a jigsaw puzzle with billions of pieces that miraculously assembles itself. But it is not exactly like a jigsaw puzzle—those pieces are merely inanimate objects. The critical components of an economy are acting human beings. It is what they do with the inanimate products such as wood or graphite or metal that results in production. The price system simply allows all these innumerable people to communicate with each other and work together. Importantly, it makes it possible for them to do this without any face-to-face contact.

It is frequently asserted that the exchange price system is unplanned and disorderly. This is completely false. It is, to the contrary, a marvel of planning and order. As Friedrich Hayek also emphasized:

> [In economics, there] is not a dispute about whether planning is to be done or not. It is a dispute as to whether planning is to be done centrally, by one authority for the whole economic system, or is to be divided among many individuals . . . [working together cooperatively].[18]

This echoes eighteenth-century economist Adam Smith's warning that it is

> folly and presumption . . . [for any] single person, . . . council or senate . . . [to try] to direct [the] employ[ment of] capital.[19]

Matt Riddley further observed in his book *Genome*, about how the human body works:

> It is the hardest thing for human beings to get used to, but the world is full of intricate, cleverly designed and interconnected systems that do not have control centers. The economy is such a system. The illusion that economies run better if someone is put in charge of them . . . has done devastating harm to the wealth and health of peoples all over the world, not just in the former Soviet Union, but in the west as well.[20]

27. *Corollary C of Law of Prices: Honest Prices* (If we want prices to do their job effectively, we must refrain from manipulating, controlling, or corrupting them.)

It is not enough to have prices. They must be honest prices. The honesty of prices is critical. In this context, honesty refers to the degree to which prices are determined by the decisions of consumers in the marketplace, or by anticipated changes in those decisions, not by merchants and others seeking to manipulate or control, usually with the help of government officials. Honest prices inform everyone about what consumers want, how much they will pay for it, and how these factors are changing. Dishonest prices convey no useful information and lead to confusion, poor decisions, or worse.

To make matters more confusing, honest prices are sometimes called "unjust" or "unfair" prices either by those sincerely wishing for better outcomes for the poor or by the parties seeking to influence or manipulate markets for their own personal gain. Interference with honest prices, including attempts to limit their ability to move up or down, may have tragic consequences.

In the eighteenth century, the price of bread was rising and peasants were starving. The French government tried to improve the situation by fixing the price of bread. Meanwhile, the cost of growing wheat was still rising, so that farmers faced growing losses. They responded logically by refusing to plant, with the result that bread became ever scarcer. It did not help the peasants to be able to buy it at a lower price when they could not buy it at all except on the black market at higher and higher prices. These kinds of mistakes were ruinous and led to the French Revolution.

Price controls were introduced long before the modern era. King Hammurabi literally carved prices in stone on a monument placed in ancient Babylon about four thousand years ago. These prices no doubt made some merchants rich and others poor. But they certainly did not reflect the underlying economic reality of the time or help provide the people of Babylon with what they most wanted at a given moment.

Dishonest and misleading prices continue to plague the global economic system. In most cases, the interference with honest pricing is disguised, so that very few people understand what is happening. The more dishonest prices are, the more harm there is to the economic system. There is a point at which dishonest prices can lead to economic collapse, as they did in Germany in the 1920s, a collapse that destroyed the German middle class and led to the rise of Hitler.

28. Corollary D of Law of Prices: (Law of) Supply (If we want to lower prices, the most effective way to do so is not to try to control them, but rather to increase supply.)

All else being equal or the same, an increase in the supply of a good will lower its price while a reduction in supply will increase it. Note the qualification: demand must remain the same for this to be true. This is perfectly logical. Unsold merchandise puts pressure on sellers to reduce price to attract buyers who either previously lacked the funds or did not choose to buy before. If the supply increases, there will by definition be more to sell and therefore more pressure to reduce price to clear the inventory.

The phrase "all else being equal" referred to above is a translation of the Latin phrase "*ceteribus paribus*" which is often used instead. All "*ceteribus paribus*" laws are qualified. They state logical tendencies or probabilities rather than absolute certainties.

29. *Corollary E of Law of Prices: (Law of) Demand* (If we want to increase prices, for example wages, the most effective way to do so is not to mandate it, but to increase demand.

This states that, again, all else being equal, an increase in buyer demand will increase prices or that in general it will tend to increase prices. This is also logical in that more buyers will be competing for the same supply of goods or the same number of buyers will be trying to buy more or buying more intensively.

30. *Corollary F of Law of Prices: (Law of) Supply and Demand* (If we allow supply and demand to operate, they will balance each other in a way that reflects consumer preferences.)

So long as an economy is primarily run by consumers, workers, and owners (who are often the same people playing different roles), their transactions naturally generate and continually update prices. The selling price of everything eventually and to the greatest degree possible balances supply and demand and reflects the most up-to-date information on factors likely to influence supply and demand as well as the latest exchange transaction data.

If consumers want less applesauce, there are fewer bidders for the product and the price will tend to fall. If consumers want more, the price may have to rise in order to persuade producers to make more.

Consumer prices in turn drive the prices for producers' goods used to make the consumer goods. In this way, consumer demand for applesauce will ultimately have some impact, however small, on the price for steel. It is a subtle but extremely powerful system.

In thinking about this, we should keep in mind that the term supply and demand are just abstractions summarizing innumerable fundamental changes. For example, bad weather may be the chief factor reducing farm commodity supply. Or something else may be involved.

Fortunately, it is not necessary for producers to understand all the fundamentals in order to decide whether to produce. They just have to know the current cost of their input factors as well as the most likely selling price. If the final selling price falls after they have already produced the product, they may have to take a loss, unless they have hedged by pre-selling.

Supply and demand are often represented in economic textbooks as lines on a graph. These are imaginary constructions since no one knows what the shapes of the curves really are at any given moment. Although arguably useful for purposes of illustration, they do not represent reality, only a concept.

31. *Corollary G of Law of Prices: (Law of) One Price* (Markets tend to produce a single price for a given good.)

In stating this, we must be careful to compare products and services that are truly comparable and interchangeable. The price of a luxury car and a more basic car will not be the same. They are two distinct products. But where goods are comparable, there will tend to be one price, because, if not, a class of entrepreneurs called arbitrageurs will buy where prices are cheap and sell where they are high, so long as transportation costs do not wipe out the potential profit.

The repeated action of reducing supply in one locale and increasing it in another to take advantage of even small price disparities will tend to create ever more uniform prices. In the nineteenth century, there was a particular active arbitrage trade in gold, because it was easy to transport, and there were profits to be made by buying it in Damascus for a little less than Cairo and then transporting it to Cairo to sell, or vice versa, even though the transportation in those days was by camel caravan.

32. *Corollary H of Law of Prices: (Law of) Marginal Utility* **(If you are trying to price your product, you cannot just take costs and add a profit margin in order to arrive at a solution. You will have to start with what the buyer will pay at this moment for this product, anticipate correctly what the buyer will pay in the near future, and then see if you can keep production costs below this figure.**

The price of a good or service at any moment is defined by what a ready, willing, and funded buyer will pay for it. If you have spent $100 building a desk and now find that no one will pay more than $50 for it, it is tough luck for you. Moreover, the amount a willing buyer will pay depends entirely on the buyer and on circumstances, both of which are constantly changing.

Price should not be confused with value. Exchanges do not take place because buyer and seller agree on the value of what is exchanged. They agree on the price only. An exchange takes place precisely because the buyer values what the seller offers more than the seller, and the seller values what the buyer offers more than the buyer. The distinction between value and price is fundamental to economics.

Economist Ludwig von Mises stressed how even a single individual's reckoning of what he or she wants (along with a feasible and acceptable price for it) is constantly shifting and will always depend on the mix of what is being bought or sold as well as the circumstances of the moment. It is always the specifics that matter. As Mises wrote in chapter XI of *Human Action*:

> The immediate goal of acting is frequently the acquisition of countable and measurable supplies of tangible things. Then acting man has to choose between countable quantities; he prefers, for example, 15 r to 7 p; but if he had to choose between 15 r and 8 p, he might prefer 8 p. . . .

> If a man exchanges two pounds of butter for a shirt, all that we can assert with regard to this transaction is that he—at the instant of the transaction and under the conditions which this instant offers to him—prefers one shirt to two pounds of butter. . . .

> Let us look at the state of economic thought which prevailed on the eve of the elaboration of the modern theory of value by Carl Menger, William Stanley Jevons, and Léon Walras. . . . The older economists [confronted] . . . a problem they failed to solve. They observed that things whose "utility" is greater are valued less than other things of smaller utility. Iron is less appreciated than gold.

[But] . . . acting man is not in a position in which he must choose between all the gold and all the iron. He chooses at a definite time and place under definite conditions between a strictly limited quantity of gold and a strictly limited quantity of iron. . . .

The law of marginal utility is already implied in the category of action. It is nothing else than [an elaboration of] . . . the statement that what satisfies more is preferred to what gives smaller satisfaction. Many other economic laws are also derived from this same premise, which in itself is nothing but a logical tautology.

The concept of marginal utility, with its stress on the constant flux of social decisions, further illustrates why it is generally not useful to graph or model economic data series.

Note Regarding Marginal Utility and Work

Many individuals work because they must do so to survive. But given a choice, most people prefer some specific combination and sequence of work and leisure. In addition, for some work will feel like a hardship endured only for its fruits and for others it will be more pleasurable than leisure.

33. *Corollary I of Law of Prices: Monopoly* (An attempt to thwart consumer power over prices tends to fail without government support. Although modern governments pretend to police monopoly, the policeman is easily bought off with protection money of one kind or another.)

The goal of a monopolist is to control supply of a good or service in order to raise or lower its price relative to a competitive free price system level. The slave owner monopolist wants to get labor for a cheap price or to ensure that he has labor without offering the necessary incentives. The business monopolist wants to be the only seller of a good that people must buy. Business monopoly only makes sense in the first place if the total revenues produced by selling less product at a higher price exceed those from selling more at a lower price. This is very difficult for a single business to achieve. For a cartel (alliance of businesses for purposes of monopoly), it may be a little easier.

Even if a single business monopoly or cartel is created, by means legal or illegal, it is extremely difficult to maintain. There will always be ingenious competitors determined to break into the business. If they cannot do so directly, they may do so indirectly by creating either a brand new production technology or another product that can be substituted for the first one. If the monopoly takes the form of a cartel, it will also find it difficult to police itself. Since the purpose of the cartel is to cheat the public, why would cartel members not try to cheat each other, for example by producing more than their allotted quota?

Over the centuries, and indeed millennia, the usual response by both slave owner monopolists and business monopolists is to enlist government as a protector. Government has the power to enforce what otherwise would quickly fail. Potential competitors will not want to risk fines or jail for daring to challenge the monopolist. Protection may take the form of statute, with violent punishments to enforce it, or less overt means. Protection money paid to government officials may either take the form of outright bribes or, more commonly today, "soft" bribes such as campaign contributions. The payments are made behind closed doors; few voters are aware of what is happening.

In the US, government laws forbid business monopolies along with restraint and restriction of trade. But if one looks more closely, the enforcement of such laws is both inconstant and inconsistent, and in many cases the government-created or -protected monopoly is not even recognized as such.

For example, a drug company pays the federal government a fee for a patent on a new drug. It then spends on average billions of dollars to take the drug through the US Food and Drug Administration (FDA) approval process. After approval, it has double monopoly protection, in that no other company can market that drug without doing the same, which it will likely not do because the opportunity for a monopoly is gone. As a direct consequence, the first company to take a drug through the approval process may charge what might be thousands of dollars for a pill that costs pennies to make. No wonder economist Milton Friedman argued that "... the most important source of monopoly power has been government assistance, direct and indirect."[21]

Chapter V

Laws of Profits

34. *Law of Profits*: **If you want lower prices for ordinary people, do not try to abolish profits. The existence of profits tends to bring prices down.**

THE POSSIBILITY OF realizing a profit (sales revenue greater than cost) continually drives down the price of goods and services.

Profits are often quite incorrectly described as an unnecessary add-on cost that increases the price of a product. This is illogical for several reasons. First, as we have discussed, it is not producer cost that sets the price of a product. Price is what buyers as a group are willing to pay. If a producer has spent more on a product than customers will pay, that produces a loss. The customer is king, and the desire of the producer to earn a profit does not itself add a penny to the price.

So far, the pursuit of profit does not add to the price. But in real life, the hope for gain is not neutral. It provides an all-important incentive for the producer to try to win over the customer. And in order to do so, the producer must offer the highest-quality goods at the lowest possible price. A business must continually improve quality and reduce price, because if it does not, a competitor will. There are exceptions to this rule, but they tend to be either rare or temporary.

Keep in mind also that, the higher profits are, the more incentive there is for entrepreneurs to produce more, which may reduce costs through economies of scale, but will also likely reduce prices through an increase in supply. If the French monarchy in the 18th century had allowed farmers to profit from growing wheat, instead of price-controlling bread, the mass starvation of peasants would have been averted, and before long the price of bread would have fallen from the increase in supply.

If both prices and profits in an industry or industry segment remain high for longer than a short time, it signals that there is some kind of economic bottleneck in the production process. For example, the bottleneck for wheat producers for centuries was protecting the grain from rodents and then getting it to market for a reasonable price. Profits lure entrepreneurs to invest to solve these problems, which in the case of wheat led to rodent-proof containers and railroad transportation.

Once a problem has been solved, and bottlenecks removed, profits tend to subside very quickly to lower and lower levels, because no competitor has an advantage over another. If there were no problems whatsoever in production, if entrepreneurs had perfect knowledge of markets as they are, agreed in their evaluation of present facts, and could forecast future consumer demand with complete accuracy, then profits over time would approach zero.

In real life, of course, none of these conditions are ever met and there are always many problems to be overcome. Some economists illogically hold that under these circumstances the free price system is imperfect. Of course it is. But it is still by far the most viable method we have of progressing under conditions of complete uncertainty. Nor does acknowledging its imperfection justify demolishing it under pretense of "improving" it.

So long as our human life remains what it is, profits in a free price system will remain above zero, but only for producers continually seeking to improve their efforts to meet the needs of customers. As this suggests, a common, expected, or "reasonable" rate of profit does not exist. In general, and importantly, the higher profits are, the more economic problems are being solved, and therefore the faster the rate of economic progress.

Economist David Ricardo said in the early 19th century that "Nothing contributes so much to the prosperity and happiness of a country as high profits."[22] Ricardo was logically correct. Why is it then that so many modern economists refuse to acknowledge this? Indeed they hardly mention the word profit, as if it embarrasses them. Economics presented in this way is a falsehood.

35. *Corollary A of Law of Profits: Consumer Control* (If you want ordinary people to control the economic system, then profits are essential for that purpose as well.)

The desire for profits provides producers with a strong incentive to serve not only consumers, but also the mass of consumers, because that is where the greatest profits are to be made. As a result, consumers as a whole not only benefit from a free price (and profit) system. They also ultimately control it. It is widely believed that capitalism is a system run by and for businesses and billionaires while socialism is a system run by and for workers. Neither formulation is correct. Real capitalism (defined as a free price system) is run by and for consumers, many of whom are also workers.

36. *Corollary B of Law of Profits: Patience* (If you are unwilling to think very long term, even beyond your lifespan, you will not be able to realize the full fruits of the profit system.)

The profit system is so demanding that most new businesses never become profitable. If they do, it may take a long time to amount to much. Eventually, however, the law of large numbers may produce surprising results.

Imagine that $10,000 in initial capital or profits grows at 12% a year, a very good rate. It will take twenty-four years to reach $160,000. In twenty more years, it will pass $2,500,000. This has essentially required a lifetime.

Britain became the leading economic power, the wonder and envy of the world, from an estimated compound economic growth rate of barely 2% a year from 1780 to 1914.[23] Two percent may not sound like much, but it was far higher than any nation had ever achieved, especially over long periods.

37. *Corollary C of Law of Profits: "Speculation"* (If you want to earn large profits, do not think that it is enough to speculate.)

There are only two ways to make a large profit in a free price system: either produce what customers want at the time and price they want it, or assist others who are doing so. It is sometimes asserted that profit making is really about "speculating" on the future and being lucky enough to get it right. There is an element of truth to this, because no one can be entirely certain about what customers and especially consumers will want, when they will want it, or what they will be willing to pay.

Keep in mind, however, that it is not only business owners who "speculate" in this way. A student who pays a large fee for an education is similarly "speculating" that it will pay off by making his services more marketable and remunerative in future years. The main point is that such "speculation" only pays if buyers eventually reward it. Buyers control, and among buyers consumers are the ultimate decision-makers.

38. *Corollary D of Law of Profits: Loss and Bankruptcy* (If you think the profit system is primarily about profit, you misread the signals it is trying to send you.)

Perhaps the single most important point to be made about the profit system is that it involves a stick as well as a carrot. It should be described as the loss and profit system, or perhaps even more accurately as the loss and bankruptcy system. Economist Wilhelm Röpke explained:

> Since the fear of loss appears to be of more moment than the desire for gain, it may be said that our economic system (in the final analysis) is regulated by bankruptcy.[24]

39. *Corollary E of Law of Profits: Change* (If you want to earn a profit, you must embrace change.)

Whether desire for profit or fear of loss (or the two together) are the motivating factor, the entrepreneur is driven to seek, embrace, and anticipate change, not just accept the status quo, and by doing so make the economy more productive. As painful as change may be, it is the process whereby we have evolved beyond living in caves, being eaten by predatory animals, and dying from the simplest injury or disability. For most of human history, the status quo has meant only abject poverty and early death for most.

The rich and powerful do not like a system that imposes penalties of loss or bankruptcy on them, and will do everything they can, including the corruption of government, to try to avoid it. Government officials are usually averse to change and thus all the more sympathetic to entreaties to try to stop it. This is inevitable and also a recurrent feature of human history.

The imperative of change in a thriving economy does not, however, apply only to entrepreneurs, business owners, or the rich and powerful. Workers who initiate change, readily adapt to it, or at least accept it will do better than those who refuse to do so.

40. *Corollary F of Law of Profits: Changing Ideas* **(Often the chief barrier to economic progress, as measured by productivity, is not scarcity of capital, skilled workers, or technology, but rather the human reluctance to give up old ideas.)**

Economist Ludwig von Mises pointed out in the introduction to *Human Action* that:

> It was the . . . [new] ideas of the . . . [eighteenth and nineteenth centuries] classical

economists that removed the checks imposed by age-old laws, customs, and prejudices upon technological improvement and freed the genius of reformers and innovators from the straitjackets of the guilds, government tutelage, and social pressure of various kinds. It was they . . . [who] reduced the prestige of conquerors and expropriators and demonstrated the social benefits derived from business activity. None of the great modern inventions would have been put to use if the mentality of the pre-capitalistic era had not been thoroughly demolished by the economists. . . .

The economists exploded the old tenets: that it is unfair and unjust to outdo a competitor by producing better and cheaper goods; that it is iniquitous to deviate from the traditional methods of production; that machines are an evil . . . ; that it is one of the tasks of civil government to prevent efficient businessmen from getting rich and to protect the less efficient against the competition of the more efficient. . . . [Without these changes, we would not have seen] . . . the progress of the natural sciences that has heaped benefits upon the masses.

41. *Corollary G of Law of Profits: "Frictional" Unemployment* ("Full employment" may signal an economy with a better past than future.)

Change by definition will bring with it at least some unemployment. Failing or status quo businesses will be laying off workers while new, innovative, or expanding businesses will be hiring. Within the United States, historically the states with the largest net job gains have also had the most job losses. The two go together in a dynamic, growing economy.

Older, less adaptable workers may suffer lasting harm from this. A caring society should not abandon them. But if there were none of this "frictional" unemployment for even temporary periods, it would imply either a stagnant economy or one blown up into an unsustainable bubble.

If there is more than temporary unemployment for most workers, or a lack of new and often better jobs to replace the lost ones, then it is not usually change that is the problem, but rather impediments to fruitful change in the form of government price controls, protection of monopoly, and other familiar features of crony capitalist reaction and corruption. Of this, more will be said in due course.

Chapter VI

Laws of Profits and Wages

42. *Law of Profits and Wages*: **If your goal is to raise wages, the price and profit system best accomplishes that.**

AS NOTED ABOVE, workers are all consumers, although not all consumers are workers. Whether workers can be said to control the price and profit system in their function as consumers will therefore depend on the ratio of workers to consumers. But workers also have a great deal of power just as workers. Marxism claimed that businesses only realized profits by exploiting workers. But this does not pass a logical test.

A business might try for a time to underpay workers in order to reduce costs or keep them down. But this business not only competes for customers. It also competes for skilled and reliable labor. If wages are too low, competitors will hire the workers away, especially the best workers.

Businesses generally find the most reliable way both to improve product quality and to lower customer price is to make productivity-enhancing investments. These investments do not generally improve profit margins, because the gains realized tend to go to employees in the form of higher wages or customers in the form of higher-quality products or lower prices. Even so, the business still stands to make more profit, because the higher-quality products or lower prices usually enable it to sell a greater volume of goods or services. More goods sold at the same or even a lower profit margin means more total profit.

43. Corollary A of Law of Profits and Wages: Union Wage Gains (If the goal is to increase the share of business revenue earned by workers, unions will not help.)

It is often assumed that wage gains won from union pressure reduce business profits. This may be true for a single business but not for the economy as a whole. The following passage from this author's book *Where Keynes Went Wrong* addresses this point and notes that union wage gains neither increase buyer demand nor decrease overall owner profits.

Who pays for union wage gains? Looking at the question from an economy-wide perspective, most of the gains of unionized workers do not come at the expense of employers' profits, as is widely thought, but rather at the expense of nonunionized workers.

In the first place, higher wages in the unionized industry mean there are fewer jobs there, so more workers compete for other nonunionized jobs and thereby reduce the wages paid for those jobs. In the second place, the products of the unionized industry generally cost more; to the degree that other industries have to buy them, those industries have less to pay workers. In addition, if workers buy the unionized product (e.g. autos), they will pay more, and thus have less money to spend on other things. If the unionized work is in government, everyone has to pay the higher price through additional taxes or through the hidden tax of inflation associated with deficit spending and printing money.[25]

44. Corollary B of Law of Profits and Wages: Mandated Wage Floors or Gains (If the goal is to help workers, these also fail their intended purpose.)

Another common misperception that the best way to fuel economic growth is to mandate higher wages, or at the very least to prevent wages from ever falling.

Both presidents Hoover and Roosevelt bought into this fallacy during the Great Depression. They agreed with journalist and philosopher Walter Lippmann that "The heart of the problem . . . [underlying the Depression has been] . . . an insufficiency of consumer . . . purchasing power."[26]

On the basis of this fallacy, they intervened with both threats and controls to prevent companies from reducing wages at a time when prices were plunging throughout the economy. The result was both predictable and tragic.

Companies faced with bankruptcy because of *de facto* and later *de jure* government wage controls at the same time that revenues were plunging began massive layoffs. Those laid off got nothing; many faced starvation. Those lucky enough to keep their jobs, in particular government employees and government-protected union members, gained an immediate financial windfall, because their wages could buy far more with consumer prices so low.

As a direct result of these policies, massive unemployment continued for a decade. By contrast, during the equally severe 1920 Depression, the government did not intervene with wage and price controls, and it was over in little more than a year. Employment quickly rebounded. The same had been true following the Panic and Depression of 1907–1908, when the economy also snapped back quickly.

During the Great Depression, economist John Maynard Keynes agreed that wage reductions would alleviate layoffs and unemployment.[27] But he wanted uniform wage reductions enforced by the government, and thought that enforcement would be too difficult. This was completely erroneous. Specific wage reductions, industry by industry, were needed, not uniform reductions, and the former could be readily accomplished by government staying out and leaving the decision to businesses.

The Great Depression happened long ago, but subsequent leaders have apparently not learned any of its lessons. In his 2014 State of the Union address, President Obama took a leaf out of Hoover's and Roosevelt's book by calling for higher minimum state and federal wages and higher wages in general: "I ask America's business leaders to raise [all] your employees' wages."

Democratic presidential candidate Hillary Clinton echoed this in a June 2016 campaign speech:

> My mission as President will be to help create more good-paying jobs so we can get incomes rising for hard-working families across America. It's a pretty simple formula: higher wages lead to more demand, which leads to more jobs with higher wages. And I've laid out a detailed agenda to jumpstart this virtuous cycle.

228 ❖ ONE HUNDRED ECONOMIC LAWS

Unfortunately, Hillary's formula is economic non-sense. If politicians think that legislating or otherwise forcing wages higher will help, why not just legislate that all wages in the US must be tripled, quadrupled, or quintupled by employers? Why stop even there?

And while at this business of raising wages by decree, why not also decree a 75% reduction in consumer prices? That would help the wage earners too, would it not? Well no, because every cost is someone's income. If either consumer prices are reduced or wage prices increased, some people, perhaps many people, will lose their jobs. If taken too far, the whole economic system will collapse.

All such moves would just throw a monkey wrench into the delicate balance of costs and prices established throughout different sectors of the economy. By doing so, they threaten profits and, in short order, cause devastating unemployment. If minimum wage laws are kept low enough, they will not precipitate another Great Depression, but they will cause some people to lose the opportunity for a job, and the hardest hit will be the young and untrained. A legislated "training" wage would mitigate this.

45. *Corollary C of Law of Profits and Wages: Say's Law of Supply and Demand* (If you want to increase demand, logically you should start by increasing supply.)

The "low demand" fallacy embraced by Hoover, Roosevelt, Obama, and Clinton is also sometimes described as the concept of "underconsumption." It was formally refuted long ago by early nineteenth-century French economist Jean-Baptiste Say.

Say argued that economies advance by increasing "supply" through profit-making ventures. If this is successful, wages will rise without interference, and demand will take care of itself. The very act of production will inevitably provide the funds to purchase what has been produced. This is not necessarily true for an individual firm, whose products may be rejected by consumers, but it will be true for the economy as a whole. John Maynard Keynes in his *General Theory* attempted to refute Say, but conspicuously failed to do so.

This explanation of Say's Law is from this author's *Where Keynes Went Wrong*:

> The idea that a society which produces will not lack the income with which to spend, with which to buy the products produced— may seem puzzling at first. It is natural to ask: What if buyers do not have the money to buy the goods produced? What then?

Fortunately the very act of production releases the money needed to buy the goods. To see why this is so, look at the following profit and loss statement for a business:

ACME PRODUCTS COMPANY	
SALES (Income)	$10,000,000
EXPENSES (Purchases)	$2,000,000
Employees	$6,000,000
Other costs	$1,000,000
Total	**$9,000,000**
Profit	**$1,000,000**

These dollars will probably not be spent on Acme products, but they will be spent on something.

Does this mean that Acme will always find a buyer for its products? Of course not. Acme will only find buyers if its products are of good quality, no more expensive than similar products, and represent something that people want. But regardless of whether people buy Acme products, there will always be money to buy them, because total economic production in an economy always generates the money necessary to buy all the products produced. The problem is not how to generate the buyers or the buying power. The problem is how to get the production going in the first place.

Wait a minute, the observant reader will say. The expenses that Acme paid out into the economy only represented 90% of its sales. What about the 10% that Acme made as profit?

The answer is that this 10% profit flows out into the economy too, although it flows out later than the expenses, and only if the Acme products are bought. Assuming that there is a profit, the owners of Acme may spend it on personal consumer goods. If not, they will save it. If they save it within the company, the company will spend it on expanding the business, and this money too will flow out into the economy where it can be used to buy something else. If the owners invest the profit outside the company, it will be spent starting or expanding another business.

The idea that (for an economy as a whole) production provides the income with which to buy its products, or, as it is often put, supply creates its own demand, is perfectly sensible when thought through. Neither Keynes nor anyone else has been able to refute it, for the simple reason that it is correct. (For a more complete explanation of why Say was right and Keynes wrong, the works of the economist W. H. Hutt are a useful resource.)[28]

Economic writer Henry Hazlitt summarized all this in the following simple terms:

> Supply creates demand because at bottom it is demand. The supply of the thing they make is all that people have, in fact, to offer in exchange for the things they want. In this sense the farmers' supply of wheat constitutes their demand for automobiles and other goods. The supply of motor cars constitutes the demand of the people in the automobile industry for wheat and other goods. All this is inherent in the modern division of labor and in an exchange economy.[29]

It is also worth noting that Say's Law refers to real prices. If nominal prices are inflated through an expansion of currency, it can cease to operate in a reliable way. We will discuss this further when we discuss money.

46. *Corollary D of Law of Profits and Wages: Balanced Prices* (If the goal is economic prosperity and more and better-paying jobs, no across-the-board price or cost adjustment will help. The key to prosperity is balancing prices in a profitable way, which can only be done price by price.)

We have already discussed why it is fallacious to think that demand drives the economy or that the most reliable way to boost demand is to force wages up or at least not let them fall. This is backward. A successful economy reliably produces handsome wage gains. Higher wages are a by-product of success, not their cause. But there are some further points to be made. This author's book *Are The Rich Necessary?* asks:

> Why are the proponents of forcing wages up so focused on wages? Do they not realize that all costs are someone's income, whether or not the cost takes the form of a wage? For example, an automobile manufacturer usually buys tires from another company. Money expended for the tire purchases is used to pay the wages of the tire manufacturer's employees. The tire manufacturer in turn buys rubber and thereby contributes to the wages of rubber company employees, and so on. Any falling price, whether

it is a wage or another price, reduces someone's nominal income, but efforts to thwart this natural process ultimately harms rather than helps workers.[30]

The fundamental reality governing all this is summarized in this author's *Where Keynes Went Wrong*:

> If an economy is stumbling, and unemployment is high, it means that some prices are far out of balance with others. Wages, for example, may be too high in relation to prices, or prices too low in relation to wages.

> Some companies, some industries may be doing well; others may be in desperate straits. What is needed is an adjustment of particular wages and particular prices within and between companies, within and between industries, within and between sectors. These adjustments are not a one-time event. They must be ongoing, as each change leads to another in a vast feedback loop.

> In some cases, the wages or other prices should rise. In other cases, they should fall. No single across-the-board adjustment will work. It will just make things worse. The economy is not a water tank to be filled or drained until the right level is reached. Such

crude plumbing will not adjust or coordinate anything. It will just make a mess.[31]

47. *Corollary E of Law of Profits and Wages: Wage Ceilings* (If wage floors do not help, might wage ceilings help, at least applied to the rich? No.)

The following example is instructive. Early in the Clinton administration, Congress passed a law limiting the corporate tax deductibility of cash compensation of chief executives of public companies to $1,000,000 a year. At first glance, this might sound reasonable. Why should such corporate leaders make more than this? But in reality, the non-deductibility of cash compensation over this figure meant that corporations stopped offering it, and instead offered stock options in lieu of the cash.

This also might sound reasonable. Stock options would tie the executive's compensation to company results, in that their option to buy the company shares at a fixed price would only be valuable if share prices went up. But it is not so simple. Although options reward executives if shares go up, they do not penalize if shares go down. As a result, if most executive compensation takes this form, managers may take risks that owners would not even consider.

Another complicating factor was that the issuance of stock options clearly cost companies money, but the Accounting Board did not require companies to acknowledge this expense. Why not? Because Congress and in particular Senator Joe Lieberman of Connecticut threatened that if they did so, Congress would strip the Accounting Board of the authority to decide these matters.

Why was Congress doing this? Because high tech and so-called dot-com companies were providing rich campaign contributions to ensure that the rules did not change. Of course Congress did not acknowledge this. They said instead that such companies were critical to the country's economic progress and therefore should not be burdened with honest accounting rules.

So, if you are a company executive, especially in tech or dot-com, what is the best way to drive your earnings and share price up and thereby make a fortune on your options? Why not borrow a lot of money and use it to buy in your shares, increasing demand for the shares while reducing supply? As we know from our discussion of demand and supply, this stands an excellent chance of increasing share prices.

Moreover, the government helps out again by allowing companies to deduct any interest costs on borrowed funds. This is in contrast to the way the government treats raising money from the sale of shares. If shares are sold and the company tries to reward the buyers with dividends, the dividend payments are taxed once at the corporate level and again at the shareholder level. This "double taxation of corporate dividends" encourages companies to finance anything they are doing with debt rather than share sales, and further encourages executives to take on more debt to buy back shares in order to make options valuable.

Providentially, from the executive's point of view, the Federal Reserve was also holding interest rates down to artificially low levels during the 1990s. This meant the money borrowed to buy in shares to boost the value of options could be had for little or no interest. What a deal!

The denouement of all this was the tech/dot-com bubble of 1995–2000, which was followed by a Crash. In direct response to that Crash, the Fed reduced interest rates even lower, which resulted in the housing bubble, which blew up in 2008.

So, in summary, creating a wage ceiling for corporate CEOs, along with many other government errors, led directly to economic bubble and bust. Did that lead Congress to repeal its misjudged intervention into corporate compensation? It did not, perhaps because the more government intervenes, the more the campaign contributions flow from industry, especially Wall Street, to politicians. By 2016, Democrats in Congress were calling for further legal restrictions on corporate compensation. Evidently, they had learned nothing from the economic havoc they had created.

Chapter VII

Laws of Economic Equality and Inequality

48. *Law of Economic Equality and Inequality*: If our goal is economic equality, we must recognize that not all forms of economic equality are logically compatible.

A FREE PRICE (AND PROFIT) system promotes both equality under the law and equality of opportunity. We must take care in thinking about equality of opportunity. It should not, for example, be confused, as it sometimes is, with equal education.

At its very best, education can only teach us how things were done in the past or are being done now. The more years of schooling, the more prestigious the schools, the more investment of time and money in establishing educational "credentials," the less likely young people may be to defy convention, to take risks, or to strike out in new entrepreneurial directions.

A degree from Harvard, Oxford, or *L'Ecole Normale Superieur* has never been a predictor of notable achievement. And, as economist Thomas Sowell has pointed out, nothing, including education, can ever level the playing field for a child born with brain damage or to abusive parents.

Although it may not be perfectly equal, there will always be opportunity in a world controlled by consumers looking for the best products at the most reasonable price. As previously noted, no one, no matter how rich or powerful, can take their current privileges for granted so long as such a system prevails. Newcomers with better ideas or more energy may at any time claim old markets or create new ones. Established elites find their position all too precarious, which leads to crony capitalist efforts to buy protection from government.

This kind of equality of opportunity requires incentives and is logically incompatible with equality of outcome. If new ideas, initiative, or hard work are not rewarded, opportunity by definition does not exist. Even if society does not want equality of opportunity, any attempt to embrace or especially enforce equality of outcome will result in inescapable contradictions.

For example, if one person takes what is initially an equal economic share and enhances it in some way, will society take it away or somehow provide it to everyone, over and over, as often as needed? How would this actually be accomplished? And why would anyone keep trying to improve their situation or that of society?

What about the fact that we are all different? If society insists on the same drug being provided for the same illness, what if the chosen drug kills some people rather than treating them, and how can we be sure it is the same drug or the same illness in the first place?

If we must all have exactly the same income, who will be included in the calculation, every person on earth, including those living on a few dollars a day, or only members of our own specific "tribe"? Most equalitarians ignore these inconvenient questions.

The French Revolution coined the famous slogan: "liberty, equality, fraternity." But it is also true that liberty and equality (of result) are logical opposites. If we give people freedom, some will use it in ways that make them materially better off, while others will choose not to do so, sometimes for poor reasons, sometimes, as in the case of religious leaders, for excellent reasons.

If we try to resolve this dilemma by enforcing equality of outcome under threat of guns and jail, we cannot possibly preserve liberty. And how can we claim that the enforcers of equality, the ones with the legal right to use guns and jails, are still equal to the rest of us? And how long should we expect those enforcers to abstain from using their power for personal, material advantage? Studies have shown that the greatest economic inequality ever recorded was in 20th-century Communist countries, run by the same kleptocrats who pledged eternal fealty to principles of economic equality of outcome.[32]

Political leaders who espouse equality of result or at least condemn what they regard as excessive and unnecessary inequality of result often contradict themselves in a variety of ways. For example, many favor government lotteries that largely take money from those who can ill spare it in order to make someone else fabulously rich. Government lotteries do not offer a larger number of small prizes for a simple reason: this does not sell tickets. Even smaller prizes will still just take money from the many and give it to the few.

The same advocates of equality of outcome may also favor open borders—although new immigrants generally increase national income inequality. This is both because the new migrants usually start out very poor and also because they usually increase the supply of unskilled labor, which tends to reduce wage growth.

President Obama, when asked if he would favor higher capital gains taxes, even if the government received less revenue as a result (something that has happened in the past), replied that, yes, he would.[33] But when owners of assets hold on to them to avoid capital gains tax, there are more serious consequences than government losing tax revenue. Perhaps the worst one is that the money cannot be rechanneled into new investments, and it is the average wage earner who is likely to suffer most from the resulting loss of economic growth. In addition, at the same time the president and vice president were expressing their deep and presumably sincere opposition to income inequality, they and their families did not hesitate to schedule vacations costing the taxpayers many millions of dollars.

It is perhaps best to put aside such interesting but irresolvable debates about what happened in the Soviet Union or why public officials take the often contradictory positions they do. Logic suggests that the most relevant question is not how we might root out inequality of income and outcome, but rather how we might ensure that everyone in society has enough.

49. Corollary A of Law of Economic Equality and Inequality: The Problem of Envy (If our goal is a better economic outcome, envy will make it harder to achieve.)

As paradoxical as it may sound, even emotions may possess an interior logic related to their usefulness. They may give us energy or devotion; they may help us respond to an emergency. Among emotions, envy is somewhat anomalous. As eighteenth-century economist and philosopher David Hume pointed out above in our discussion of comparative advantage, it is hard to find a useful purpose for envy. If someone else prospers in a system of honest prices, it does not harm me. On the contrary, it means this person can now afford to buy more from me, if I can figure out what that person might need or value and meet that need.

As Hume further noted, what is true for two people or two groups of people is equally true for two countries. The rational approach is not to begrudge the prosperity of our neighbors, but rather to wish them well and to seek to benefit from their prosperity, in keeping with the laws of the division of labor and of comparative advantage.

50. *Corollary B of Law of Economic Equality and Inequality: Inequality "Data" and Its Interpreters* (If we try to illuminate these matters with data, it takes a great deal of careful thought to ensure that it is not irrelevant or even misleading. With information, as with production or investment, the most critical issue is quality, not just quantity.)

Various economists have long sought to demonstrate that rising inequality is an unavoidable feature of a free price system. None of them have succeeded. The most recent, French economist Thomas Piketty, floated the thesis that investments made by the rich must inevitably outpace the earnings growth of everyone else. This is supposed to be baked in the cake, unavoidable, but we are given no real argument to support it. Instead, we are presented with what he calls "spectacular" charts purporting to show investment returns from thousands of years ago and in particular steadily rising inequality for the last century.

All of this is nonsense. If the rich had really earned the high returns claimed for thousands of years, they would own infinite multiples of today's global investment assets or economic output.

A close look at the charts covering more recent history reveals that the top 10% earners (not the true rich) have increased their share of income, but only during economic bubble periods such as the 1920s, the late 1990s, and the period leading to the Crash of 2008. Such bubbles in reality are symptomatic of dishonest, not honest prices, of crony capitalism, not capitalism, as will be discussed later. In addition, most of the relative gains made by the top 10% were given back after the bubbles popped. There is no evidence of a sustained rise.

In addition, common sense suggests that production for the masses, which makes the rich truly rich, improves the living standards of the masses more than anybody else. Comforts and amenities that were once only available for the rich are now commonplace, even in less developed countries.

Data on economic inequality from other sources, such as the US government, may be a little more credible than

Piketty's, but still suffers from numerous flaws. For example, income data is collected by household rather than by individual, so that changes in the average size of households affect the numbers in hard-to-calculate ways. Some government benefits are included while others are excluded for no apparent reason other than statistical gaming.

Recent immigrant data is not broken out, even though immigrants often start out in the bottom quintile of income. Differences in hours worked are ignored. Capital gains are treated as income, although economically they represent an exchange of one existing asset for another, not true economic income, and so on.

51. *Corollary C of Law of Economic Equality and Inequality: Greed and Conspicuous Consumption* **(If our goal is economic equality of opportunity rather than of outcome, this does not in any way condone "greed.")**

To say that a goal of equality of outcome involves inescapable logical contradictions and that a goal of "enough" for all would be more rational does not in any way endorse or defend economic greed. As noted above, a free price (and profit) system rewards those who serve the largest numbers of others by providing the best possible products at the lowest possible price.

Greed may seem to be a successful policy in the short run, but rarely produces the greatest amount of profit over time. As the eighteenth-century economist Adam Smith shrewdly observed, the pursuit of profit actually regulates "selfishness and rapacity," because these vices drive away both employees and customers. Economist Israel Kirzner's remark: "The essential quality of a market system is not that it promotes greed, but that it renders greed harmless," is only a half-truth, because the market system actually penalizes the greedy.[34]

Everyone in the free price system has a job to do. The job of the rich is not to outdo each other in greed or in conspicuous and empty displays of competitive consumption. It is to live modestly and efficiently so that unspent income may be channeled into wise investments. Saving, converting savings into wise investments for society as a whole, and managing these investments (or at least overseeing this process) is the main job. It is even better when the rich also give to charities, and better still when they take responsibility for managing them. As John Wesley, the founder of the Methodist Church, put it pithily in a sermon: "Having gained all you can, save [in order to invest] all you can, and give all you can."[35]

Only the rich can play the critical role of investor for society. The poor and middle class lack the surplus income with which to invest. Government lacks the knowledge and experience, is unable to look beyond immediate political considerations, and will invariably spend whatever income it has or more. We all spend and invest more carefully if we are using our own money.

Government is always spending someone else's money and has virtually unlimited means to do so. Under these circumstances, it is up to the rich to make investment decisions for the entire economy, guided and disciplined by the price signals received from consumers. If they do this job poorly, consumers will let them know by inflicting losses or even bankruptcy.

52. Corollary D of Law of Economic Equality and Inequality: The "Trickle Down" Fallacy (We need not fear that the success of the rich will impoverish the poor.)

Returning to Say's Law for a moment, the flow of funds described within it helps reveal a logical flaw in the core concept of "trickle down," the notion that a free price system acts as Robin Hood in reverse by taking from the poor and middle class and giving to the rich. According to this fable, the poor and middle class have to make do with the few crumbs that fall from the rich person's table.

In real life, the rich use their savings to make an investment. The investment may be in plant or equipment or labor, but the money will immediately flow out into the economy where it will be used, directly or indirectly, to pay wages. If, and only if, the investment succeeds, the original capital is returned to the rich along with an additional increment in the form of profit. Whatever portion of the profit is saved will again flow out in investment and so on. Since investment flows to workers first, before returning to the investor, if it ever does return, it is false to claim that the system "trickles down" or is set up to despoil the poor and middle class.

53. *Corollary E of Law of Economic Equality and Inequality: Wealth Taxes* (If you want to help the poor or middle class, do not tax wealth.)

Wealth taxes on the rich are one of the principal recommendations of economist Thomas Piketty. This is a very bad idea. As noted above, the entire economy depends on the quality and quantity of investments by the rich. Taxing their income, or taxing their personal expenditures, will not promote economic growth or job creation, but it will do far less harm than destroying capital investment by taxing wealth.

If accumulated wealth is not re-invested, the most logical place for it to go is into charity. A national charity ran a tongue-in-cheek ad titled "Five Reasons Not to Make a Will," one of which read:

> The government will use your estate tax dollars more efficiently than your favorite charity would use a charitable bequest.[36]

As this suggests, no one believes that government is efficient in its expenditure of funds for social relief (or other purposes).

There is a further logical problem with taxing wealth. Although it is possible to tax some wealth through property taxes or inheritance taxes, taxing larger amounts would require a massive sale of stocks, bonds, and real estate by the rich owners of these assets. In this case, there would be few or no buyers to absorb the sales, so that market values would collapse.

Because markets anticipate, the collapse would actually precede the tax due date, thereby eliminating the very wealth the government expects to tax. In addition, businesses, anticipating the choking off of saving and investment, would stop investing, which would precipitate massive layoffs. For all these reasons, the taxing of capital on a large scale is more likely to impoverish everyone than to enrich the government or improve the lives of those who have the least.

54. *Corollary F of Law of Economic Equality and Inequality: Wealth "Redistribution"* (It is not advisable, but there are better and worse ways to do it.)

Wealth "redistribution" poses a variety of problems. The usual method is for government to tax the income of the rich at higher rates than others. This is less destructive than a wealth tax, but still reduces investment capital (because less is left after tax) as well as the incentive to invest, produce, and re-invest. It also hits the rising rich harder, because they have less capital already in hand for their investments, and rely more heavily on after-tax income savings to provide it.

Producers who find that they are in effect working many long months for the government rather than for themselves or their families, after the income tax has taken its toll, will also think twice about risking the capital they have already accumulated net of tax. The combination of less investment, fewer incentives, and less risk-taking reduces potential future income for investor and worker alike.

None of this can be accurately captured by statistics. For one thing, income taxes do not exist in isolation. The rates matter, in that higher rates are much more damaging to economic potential, but everything matters. One study that has attempted to measure impact found that each $1 of tax on the private sector reduced economic production by $2.25, notwithstanding any increase in economic demand from the government spending.[37]

In thinking about how all this works, we must recognize that production and distribution, which Marxist terminology arbitrarily separates into two unconnected logical categories, are in real life part of the same, seamless process. They are just different aspects of the same thing. If we interfere with the distribution of income determined by supply and demand (and expressed in free prices), we also interfere with production, and should expect to reduce it.

This leads to the familiar quip that socialism succeeds in creating equality of income, but only by impoverishing us all. This is not actually accurate, because, as noted above, no matter how impoverished most people become, the rulers of the equality system will always be superior to others, not only in power, but also in income.

Another problem with conventional methods of income "redistribution" is that the money does not go directly from rich to poor, but is instead diverted into government, which at best takes its toll and at worst consumes all of it. Over the years, much of the money ends up paying for very good livings for government employees, most of whom cannot even be fired for failure to perform. It is easy for the government employees running social programs to think they are helping others when, in fact, they are helping themselves.

Perhaps even worse, the money that is "redistributed" may be utilized as a vote-buying scheme. It is all too easy for government to collect extra taxes on the rich, use it to pad its own lifestyle, and then drop a few crumbs to the poor in return for their regular vote.

If democratic voters really want to "redistribute" income, at whatever cost to their own future material welfare, there are more realistic and therefore better ways to do it. An alternative would be to legislate a single tax rate applicable to everyone that would be intended to provide necessary government revenue. Beyond that, there could be a surtax on the rich, but the rich could avoid it by giving the sum in question to social service charities and taking a 100% tax credit when they do so.

Such a tax credit would produce a gusher of money going to social service charities and ensure competition between them for the money. Charities doing a good job would receive more of the available funds from donors; charities doing a bad job would receive less or none. In this way, government could remove itself from the business of deciding who gets what, and also from the temptation to seek to buy votes this way.

This method is described in more detail in this author's book *Are The Rich Necessary?* The goal is to reform what is now a highly corrupt and inefficient government social service system by introducing tried and true principles of competition.

55. *Corollary G of Law of Economic Equality and Inequality: Making the Worker the Boss* (Employee ownership as a potential way to "redistribute" income more broadly is also problematic.)

The free price system is a system based on change. The composition of the workforce of any business is part of this change. The respective contributions of employees are also changing, often dramatically. To try to build the ownership of a business on the shifting sands of today's employees is to invite instability and unsustainability. Moreover, most businesses need capital over and above what they can retain from earnings after tax, and workers cannot be expected to supply such capital.

Chapter VIII

Laws of the Division of Labor within the Free Price System

56. *Summary Law of the Division of Labor within the Free Price System*: If we wish to be economically successful and prosperous, we must choose competition within an overall framework of cooperation, and in doing so, reject other choices, such as tribalism.)

EVERY SOCIETY OF living organisms, even microorganisms, reveals a mixture of self-sacrifice, cooperation, competition, and parasitism. These are the basic choices; they are our basic choices. The human race for most of its history was organized into tribal groups that cooperated with each other while ruthlessly preying on members of other tribes. Aggression, hatred, cruelty, murder, annihilation, envy, theft, lust for the few material possessions in existence, even or especially lust for slaughter were all discouraged intra-group, but promoted extra-group.

Economist Ludwig von Mises and others have pointed out the illogic of this system. But there was originally a kind of primitive logic to it. Material possessions were very scarce; the most reliable way to get them was murder and theft. In addition, and even more importantly, fear of and ferocity toward enemy tribes was the glue that held each tribe together. Without an outside enemy, the tribe might fall apart.

Very, very small groups of early humans cooperated just to eke out bare survival. They had savage enemies in the form of predatory animals as well as what was often a very harsh environment. But once groups got larger than a few dozen people, there was nothing more likely to hold them together than fear and hatred of other groups. Historian and prominent newspaper columnist Joseph Alsop described this basic system of shared tribal aggression in the 1960s:

> What do we need in America to endure? It isn't enough to say that we are very numerous, or that we are vastly rich in proportion to everyone else in the world. Being that rich simply makes us a target, if you think about it. Everybody else would like to divide up our goods. They'd like to chew us up like a dead whale on a beach, if we'd let them do

> it. And I have the warmest sympathy for
> that desire. It is perfectly understandable,
> and we mustn't complain about it.[38]

Such tribal thinking and behavior may be entirely
understandable, since it has been the norm for all of
human history, but there are other and better alternatives, including larger-scale models of cooperation, or
even better, competition within an overall framework
of larger-scale models of cooperation.

57. *Corollary A of Summary Law of the Division of Labor within the Free Price System: Competition within an Overall System of Cooperation* (This necessarily produces superior economic results relative to either competition or cooperation alone.)

What exactly is meant by competition within an overall framework of cooperation? At the simplest level,
we see it in a pickup basketball or touch football game.
The participants are all cooperating with each other.
By doing so, they experience the joys of movement,
of exercise, and of camaraderie. They have fun. Dividing up into two teams makes it more fun, because the
cooperation now has a structure and a goal.

In business, it is not necessarily about fun, although
there is enjoyment to be had. As in sports, the competition is ultimately cooperative in nature. It is not

a war of annihilation of one group against another. It is a system of teams whose goal is to provide the best products and services to consumers at the lowest possible price. For the system to flourish, there must be cooperation inside the competing teams, but even the competing teams are cooperating by sharing a common goal and by observing the rules of the game.

Sometimes competitors do not even realize they are competitors. Wheat farmers are competitors, but the market is so large in relation to anyone's sales that producers tend to see each other as colleagues, not as rivals. In other industries, competition is direct, fierce, even cutthroat, but the players must still observe the rules. If they refuse to do this, if, for example, they violate the "nonaggression axiom" by initiating the use of violent force, steal, or commit fraud, they pay, and deserve to pay, substantial penalties, which, in addition to losses or bankruptcy, may include jail.

58. *Corollary B of Summary Law of the Division of Labor within the Free Price System: Growing Networks* (There is no limit to the number of people who can simultaneously compete and cooperate in this way.)

A growing network of exchange is unconstrained by communication and other barriers. Prices are the common language which everyone can understand. For the first time in history, all human beings can be connected with each other and learn to depend on each other. As labor is divided among larger and larger numbers, the opportunity for creating wealth and overcoming poverty just keeps expanding with the network.

59. Corollary C of Summary Law of the Division of Labor within the Free Price System: Worldliness Redefined (Aggression no longer pays.)

Where once the worldly policy was predation, or at best parasitism, to some degree tempered by religion, but also sometimes fanned by it, now the worldly policy is to treat other human beings with consideration and respect, if only to sell them our products. As we get to know distant people, softer sentiments may also begin to flow. Our children may inter-marry. But softer sentiments only have an opportunity to arise because a system of mutual cooperation brings us together in the first place. This is a truly revolutionary change, albeit one still largely unrealized and still fiercely opposed by many powerful factions and world governments today.

60. *Corollary D of Summary Law of the Division of Labor within the Free Price System: Nation Size* (In this new world, with respect to political units, "small is beautiful.")

From the point of view of world peace, or at least avoiding mass annihilation, the best plan for the human race would be to cooperate through one world market while keeping nation states as small as possible, each too small to threaten its neighbors. A world comprised of only Switzerlands and Singapores all cooperating together through trade would seem to be the ideal.

Tiny nation states cooperating in a global world economy would also persuade even the most ambitious would-be empire builders that the commerce represents a far better prospect than war. As eighteenth-century English thinker and wit Samuel Johnson noted: "There are few ways in which a man can be more innocently employed than in getting money."[39]

Tiny states would also make it easy for anyone disillusioned with his own to move to another near or far. Because these states would not like to lose their population, especially their more productive citizens, they would be forced to compete for citizens by providing a better environment and political climate.

61. *Corollary E of Summary Law of the Division of Labor within the Free Price System: Individualism and Cooperatism* (Contrary to common assumption, the two are actually synonymous.)

This irony is remarked on by economist Ludwig von Mises:

> The customary terminology misrepresents these things entirely. The philosophy commonly called individualism is a philosophy

of social cooperation and the progressive intensification of the social nexus. On the other hand, the application of the basic ideas of collectivism [tribalism] cannot result in anything but social disintegration and the perpetuation of armed conflict.

All varieties of collectivist creeds are united in their implacable hostility to the fundamental political institutions ... [promoted by the free price] system: majority rule, tolerance of dissenting views, freedom of thought, speech, and the press, equality of all . . . under the law. This collaboration of collectivist creeds in their attempts to destroy freedom has brought about the mistaken belief that the issue in present-day political antagonisms is individualism versus collectivism. In fact it is a struggle between individualism on the one hand and a multitude of collectivist sects on the other hand whose mutual hatred and hostility is no less ferocious than their abomination of the . . . [free price] system. . . .[40]

In Mises's day, tribal creeds also looked more alike in that virtually all of them promised the same benefits offered by the free price system: limitless material prosperity and eventual conquest of poverty. Today we have been reminded of what history should have taught us: that tribal creeds may take a completely different tack and operate on nihilist and terrorist principles intended to undermine and eventually destroy material civilization.

62. *Corollary F of Summary Law of the Division of Labor within the Free Price System: World Governments Today* (Not only nihilist terrorist organizations, but also national governments, especially the world's "great powers," continually threaten to pull us back into atavistic and destructive tribalism.)

Primitive, tribal aggression has always been the basic model for governments. Rulers promise to share what is stolen from others. Most of all, they try to distract the ruled from their own misrule by picking quarrels with outside tribal groups.

In the modern era, the language of aggression has been sublimated. No ruler today wants to sound like Genghis Khan. And there are many different nuances of method.

The leader may (a) seek to unite one country against an alleged foreign enemy or enemies, (b) unite some groups against others within a country to create an electoral majority, (c) preach unity except before elections or during crises that may topple the rulers, (d) rely on tribal methods within the country while condemning tribalism outside it.

Of the latter approach, columnist Charles Krauthammer had this critique of President Barrack Obama:

> For all the embrace of identity politics at home, abroad Obama has preached the opposite. Here is a man telling a black audience in September that he would "consider it a personal insult, an insult to my legacy" if they don't turn out for the Democratic candidate in November. Yet on his valedictory tour abroad just nine weeks later, he lectures anyone who will listen . . . to resist the siren song of "a crude sort of nationalism, or ethnic identity, or tribalism." This is rather ironic, given that what was meant as a swipe at . . . ethno-nationalism is a fairly good description of the Democratic Party's domestic strategy of identity politics.[41]

We cannot expect politicians to foreswear tribalism so long as it works with the voters. But as noted above, where tribalism was once an inescapable reality with its own interior (if always warped) logic, that is no longer the case. Human cooperation is no longer strictly limited by geography and primitive communication; all the barriers have fallen.

Technology and especially the free price system have changed everything. They enable us not only to cooperate globally, but even better, to compete peacefully within an overall framework of cooperation. By doing so, we can gain far, far more than from predation or other forms of "us-against-them" aggression.

Nineteenth-century historians developed what some called "the Whig theory of history." This held that the human race was steadily progressing from failed systems of coercion and corruption to ones of fruitful cooperation. The horrors of the world wars and Communist gulags that followed put this idea to rest. But the great promise of moving from coercion and corruption to global cooperation remains. Whether the human race will grasp the opportunity remains to be seen.

Chapter IX

Laws of Economic Calculation

63. *Law of Economic Calculation*: If we wish to succeed economically, we must take full advantage of economic calculation.

HUMAN BEINGS ARE naturally impatient with all forms of discipline. But we need them for our own good. Markets reflecting free and honest prices provide both discipline and opportunity. To benefit from the discipline and to take advantage of the opportunity, we must pay assiduous attention to economic calculation. Refusal to pay heed to this law commonly leads to economic failure, even bankruptcy. This is true for individual businesses but also societies.

Computing assets, liabilities, expenses, revenues, profits and changes in these series is essential. Every detail must be patiently scrutinized. If our costs are too high, our revenues too low, or our capital inadequate, the sooner we acknowledge the problem the better off we will be. Remaining in denial will not make reality kinder.

With the exception of science and technology, nothing has so benefited the human race as double-entry bookkeeping, accounting conventions, and all the related tools. As prosaic or humdrum as these tools may seem, they are magical in their ability to organize the division of labor in more and more productive ways.

It should be acknowledged that, in some respects, the tools of economic calculation are defective. As numerically exact as each calculation must be, it nevertheless represents only a best guess of the underlying economic reality. The depreciated value of a truck is shown at X on the asset side. But is it really worth X if sold? Perhaps not. In addition, as soon as calculations are made, they are outdated. They describe a past that has come and gone.

Somewhat paradoxically, these guesstimated and backward-looking analyses nevertheless enable us to plan and decide for the future. Whatever their imperfections, they give entrepreneurs the confidence to make reasonable bets. Nothing about the social or economic past can reliably predict the future, but accurate figures illuminate what would otherwise be a grope in the dark. In addition, once the bet has been made, the numbers tell us how it is working out, and often give us time to correct course, either to achieve a better outcome or to avert calamity.

64. *Corollary A of Law of Economic Calculation: Measuring Change* (As noted earlier, if the goal is economic progress, change is inescapable, and economic calculation is the essential tool to manage and promote intended rather than unintended change.)

Economic calculation is a critical tool to help us cope with, but also facilitate and benefit from, change. The more economic calculation there is, the more chance that change can be channeled into intentional, purposeful, constructive projects that both meet personal objectives and also help contribute to social objectives such as ending poverty or protecting the environment.

Because government is not directly disciplined by consumers operating in a marketplace, as businesses are, it is easier for public officials to deny failure and much easier to evade or at least postpone bankruptcy. As previously noted, this can mean that government becomes the chief obstacle to economic change of any kind. This is especially true when it has been captured by special interests opposed to change because it threatens their own vested interests or elite status.

65. *Corollary B of Economic Calculation: Limits of Calculation* (As in everything else, it is quality of economic calculation, and attention to its limits, that matters most. Net present value offers an especially helpful perspective in that it keeps us focused on the long term, not just backward-looking financial statements.)

Many important inputs into social and economic action cannot be expressed in prices and therefore cannot be calculated. These include such personal qualities as honesty, integrity, character, reliability, dedication, energy, even health, but also such elements as beauty of design or convenience of use. It can be argued that what matters most in life, including economic life, is not calculable in this way.

In addition, economic calculation can give us the quantities of our investments, but there will be a considerable period of time before it provides feedback on the quality of these choices, and in human life it is always quality, not quantity, that matters most. We cannot expect to advance economically if we do not save and accumulate capital. At the same time, as Ludwig von Mises observed, capital itself does not "beget" profit, only wisely invested capital can accomplish that. We will revisit these observations again when we come to the causes of business cycles.

The nature of financial statements, with their focus on numbers from one date, may also lead us to put too much emphasis on the here and now, which is really already gone, rather than on the future. But other calculations, such as computing the possible net present value* of our investments helps remedy this potential defect.

In a simpler economy, owners of capital generally make and tend their own investments. This has many advantages, because no one has more incentive to succeed than the owner. In our more advanced economy, the owners often necessarily rely on hired managers. Because the managers know so much more about what is happening than the owner, the latter could easily be deceived if economic calculation did not cut to the heart of the matter, whether a profit is being made.

It can be particularly problematic when managers share in profits without sharing in losses, as we have discussed in the context of stock options. This can create an incentive for the manager to take greater risk than the owner would, because the personal reward is not balanced by personal risk.

In our world of such complete uncertainty, economic calculation only does so much for us, but it gets us through, and gives us the confidence needed to take actions that may improve our position.

---

* Net present value calculations take our best guess of future cash flows and discount them back to present value using some discount rate, computed by adding an interest rate with a risk adjustment factor. In this way, we can compare future cash flows with today's cash and consider the longer term, not just what is immediate.

66. *Corollary C of Law of Economic Calculation: Externalities* (For society to make best use of economic calculation, we must understand this limitation in particular.)

Some economic inputs or outputs are calculable, but are not conventionally captured in accounting costs. A notorious example is pollution created by a factory. If the owner of a factory can pollute without economic penalty, there is a great temptation to do so, and even to rationalize the behavior as socially responsible, which it is not.

The tendency to create externalities is exacerbated by the economic principle that property owned by "everybody," such as air or rivers or oceans, will often be neglected or abused, unlike property owned by somebody, which has calculable value.

This is rightly considered a flaw in the system of economic calculation. If it were easy to fix, it would long since have been fixed, but there are reasons to think that the problem lies in the surrounding framework of laws rather than in economic calculation itself.

Over the centuries, the tort legal system has been developed in Anglo-Saxon countries in particular to handle such challenges. If a factory moves next door to my house and fouls my air, I can sue for damages, which will certainly monetize the pollution. But government has often been allied with the polluter, which makes it difficult to get justice in court. In addition, legal costs are usually prohibitive for all but the very rich. Public interest law firms representing plaintiffs help to alleviate this problem, but are not generally well-funded.

As confidence in the tort system has waned, direct government regulation of pollution has waxed. Such direct regulation can be effective, but it is a blunt instrument, it requires an unrealistic degree of technical expertise on the part of government, and it pulls government into the minutiae of running the economy. It also gives the polluting industry a huge incentive to try to buy favor with government through campaign donations and other favors. The end result is pollution of government as well as of the environment.

In recent decades, the idea of taxing externalities has become ever more popular. For example, if the tobacco industry is creating an externality of ill health, which in turn leads to enormous public and private health expenditure, then just tax the cigarettes to recoup these costs. The higher cost of the product with the added tax will also discourage its sale.

But that is just the problem. Governments can very easily become dependent on sin or pollution tax revenues. If so, this creates a perverse incentive for government to encourage the externality or at least protect the industry rather than its victims. In the case of the cigarette industry, the government has benefited from legal settlements funding itself and its cronies as well as high tax revenues. As a result, it has created a cigarette cartel protecting the cartel members from competition. Both logic and evidence suggest that sin or externality taxes too easily backfire and should therefore be avoided.

What has not yet been tried is a legal approach to externalities that requires polluting companies, not to pay taxes to government, but rather to invest in companies or fund non-profits charged with cleaning up pollution. Safeguards would have to be constructed to help ensure that there is real competition among potential recipients of these funds, not just a scramble by government cronies to collect them, so the details of the legal arrangement would matter a great deal. The objective would be to impose a calculable financial penalty by law, but to keep these funds out of government itself, so that it does not have a direct stake in the continuation of the undesirable externality.

Meanwhile externalities remain a potential loophole in the otherwise tightly organized system of economic calculation.

Chapter X

Laws of Economic Calculation outside Business

67. *Law of Economic Calculation outside Business*: Whatever its limitations outside of business, it is still the essential tool.

E CONOMIC CALCULATION MIGHT sound like business calculation when described as book-keeping and accounting, but it applies to non-profit enterprises and governments as well. A non-profit may not seek profits, but can easily go bankrupt, especially if it takes on debt. The same is true of government, which can also end up bankrupt, acknowledged or otherwise.

Granted, the nature of calculation is very different for a business versus a non-profit or a government. Businesses must weigh not only what it pays for its inputs, the goods or services it must buy. It must also try to discern from current prices what customers might be willing to pay for its output and must pay a heavy penalty for getting it wrong. Non-profits in most cases and government in all cases lack such direct guidance from customers, but still must grapple with assets and liabilities, revenues and expenses. In all these cases, economic calculation is still essential.

For example, assume that a government is trying to decide between building a road, a bridge, a prison, or a school, or hiring more police. How can it possibly weigh the advantages and disadvantages of each expenditure without even knowing what the expenditure might be? It is not uncommon for governments to ignore this calculation or try to manipulate it, but this will just result in a poor decision.

68. Corollary A of Law of Economic Calculation outside Business: "Borrowed Prices" (In order for a government to calculate, it must "borrow" prices.)

When government estimates the cost of building a bridge, it relies on, that is, it "borrows" prices ultimately established by consumers in the marketplace. In addition, by adding its own demand to the equation, it also changes those prices.

This is workable if the government is not the primary source of demand and thus the price setter. But when government becomes the primary source of demand, or especially the only source of demand, then the market price system is no longer a market price system. It cannot be expected to provide the same vital feedback loop about what market participants need to complete their projects efficiently or want for themselves and what they will pay for it.

Under these circumstances, government may try to fill the vacuum by stepping in to define and dictate what supply, demand, or prices will be, but it will not work any better than it did when the French government tried to price control bread, described above. Without honest prices that balance the genuine needs and wants of all producers and consumers, in a way that is ultimately controlled by consumer demand, the system will eventually disintegrate.

The disintegration of the Soviet experiment illustrates this. The system limped along by "borrowing" from market economies elsewhere in the world, but that was only a stopgap and could not prevent gross misallocation of capital and growing inefficiency.

As Ludwig von Mises, the first economist to point out the impossibility of economic calculation under socialism, noted:

> It is not enough to tell a man not to buy on the cheapest market . . . [assuming comparability

of product and product quality] and not to sell
on the dearest market. . . . One must establish unambiguous rules for the guidance of
conduct in each concrete situation.[42] . . .
And no alleged "fact finding" and no arm-
chair speculation can discover a . . . price
at which demand and supply . . . will become equal.[43]

69. Corollary B of Law of Economic Calculation outside Business: Halfway Houses between Socialism and a Free Price System (If we mix Socialism with the Free Price System, we should not expect optimal results.)

A socialist system cannot solve the problem of economic calculation. Many socialists argue that their system has never been given a fair chance because previous
historical experiments were half-baked or insincere, but
this does not matter for our analysis, which is based on
logic rather than historical evidence.

It is equally true that a pure free price system has
not yet been attempted, much less achieved, in any
country either now or in history. But logic and experience both indicate that free prices solve the economic calculation problem, not perfectly but to a
remarkable degree. What then happens when the
two systems are joined together, some of one and
some of the other?

Such mixed systems represent an attempt to combine logical opposites and are therefore no more sensible than trying to create a triangular square. We should not expect to produce the most optimal results from such an exercise. President Obama did not seem troubled by this point when he traveled to Cuba and asserted that there was not that much difference between capitalism and communism. There is a sense in which he is right, because both the American and Cuban communist systems have been mixed, just in different ways.

It is not, however, true that one mixed system will be as productive as another. Insofar as the system mostly protects the free and honest prices underlying genuine economic calculation, it should do better. Insofar as it does not, it should do worse, experience increasing failure, and end in crisis. Since failure by its nature is neither stable nor sustainable, it will tend to generate pressures for further change, but this more often than not just means doubling down on the mistakes that led to the crisis.

Because the nature of the underlying illogic is rarely understood, the usual call will be for the government to "do something" about the failures, which will just lead to more government intervention in the price system, fewer honest prices, less genuine economic calculation, and even greater failure, in a potentially disastrous downward spiral. Many societies have followed this path, including most notoriously, the late Roman Empire.

In our own day, economists are sometimes among the most ardent advocates of government tinkering with and ultimately taking apart the consumer price system and thus abandoning genuine economic calculation. They do this for a variety of reasons, mercenary or sincere, but often cite the primacy of "welfare" principles over "market" principles. Unfortunately, such economists have never satisfactorily demonstrated how these "welfare" principles are to be constructed or agreed upon, or why they should not be dismissed as special interest or personal pleading.

Chapter XI

Economic Law of Government

70. *Summary Economic Law of Government*: The deeper government gets into controlling the economy, the more social and economic corruption it creates.

CRITICISM OF GOVERNMENT efforts to evade or even destroy the free price system and its crown jewel of economic calculation does not mean that public officials do not have a potentially constructive role to play in the economy. They should be protecting honest prices and contracts in addition to protecting citizens against aggression and violence or threats of aggression or violence at home or from abroad. They should be the guardians of society against parasitism and predation in any form.

Because society has given public officials the control of guns, fines, and jails, among other instruments of violence and compulsion, along with virtually unlimited funds to prosecute (and in the process bankrupt) everyone, fairly or unfairly, it can be absolutely catastrophic if the guardians themselves become parasites or predators. Crony capitalism is the worm that continually gnaws at the fruit of the apple of government.

Democratic systems of government offer a somewhat greater degree of protection, if honored, in that they provide a method for removing public officials. But many a dictator has initially come into power through the ballot box. In addition, democracy represents the rule of the majority, and majorities themselves may become parasitical or predatory toward minorities. This is why it is so important for all laws to apply to everyone without exception and for no law to single out a group or groups, however defined. Finally, government must itself pay attention to its own financial calculations and continually discipline its expenditures.

Chapter XII

Laws of Money

71. *Law of Money*: If people accept and use something as money without first having to convert it to money, then it is money. It is not legal tender laws that make it money.

MONEY IS A product like any other in the economy. It provides a medium of exchange, that is, we trade a good or service for money with the objective of using that money to buy other goods or services.

Without the production of goods and services, most of what passes as money today would be meaningless. It is only because it can be converted into goods and services, and indeed is much more readily convertible into them than any other product, that we value it.

Because money comes in so many forms, it is difficult to define with exactitude. Coins and bills are money.

But so are funds in checking accounts or on credit or debit cards, so long as they are accepted as cash. Highly tradable and therefore "liquid" loans may function in a way that resembles money, but are not exactly the same. When home equity loans were first developed and you could turn your house into cash in a few hours, even houses began to function as quasi-money, but not as actual money.

72. *Corollary A of Law of Money: Gold* (Although gold today is not "legal tender," it still functions as an "alternative" currency.)

Gold or other precious metals functioned as money for at least the last five thousand years. Although we cannot reconstruct exactly how gold in particular acquired this function, it is reasonable to assume that it was widely and highly valued as a commodity before it became money, and this along with its compactness and transportability recommended it as an intermediate good, that is, a good to be held in anticipation of further exchange. The term commodity money has been applied either to gold (or another precious metal) or a certificate identifying ownership of a particular store of gold.

If the certificate records an obligation to deliver gold, but does not indicate ownership of specifically identified coins or bars, it is merely a contract and does not count as true commodity money. As gold paper contracts multiply, it is a bit like the children's game of musical chairs. At some point, the music may stop and many holders of these contracts may find there is far too little actual metal to fulfill them.

Although gold no longer has government sanctioned status as money, it is worth noting that central banks still hold what John Maynard Keynes called the "barbarous relic" in their vaults, and many are adding to those holdings. In this case, we should observe what they do, not what they say.

Because precious metals have commodity value apart from their money value, and especially because they cannot, like dollars, be endlessly replicated by government, or canceled by government (as was done on a massive scale in India in 2016), they may represent a more reliable store of future value. On the other hand, the US government under President Franklin Roosevelt seized all gold holdings of individuals in the 1930s and abrogated the gold convertibility clause in government bond contracts, so the there is always the specter of confiscation. In the 1930s at least, gold mining shares were not seized.

73. *Corollary B of Law of Money: Gresham's Law (If money is debased by government, the inferior money will tend to drive good money from circulation.)*

This was one of the very earliest formulations of an observed and predictable economic regularity. It appears in an early form in Nicholas Oresme's (c. 1357)

Treatise on Money, but the idea is as old as *The Frogs,* an ancient Greek play by Aristophanes.

The original formulation noted that when government surreptitiously clipped gold from the edge of a coin, people responded by trying to save or hoard the unclipped coins while offloading the inferior coins onto others. In this way, the good currency disappeared from circulation.

Of course, this effect will no longer operate, or operate in the same way, after all the good currency has already been taken out of circulation. It can also be retarded by "legal currency" laws compelling citizens to accept inferior money mandated by government.

74. Corollary C of Law of Money: "Paper" Money (Given that "paper" money has even less gold in it than a clipped or diluted coin, and as noted above is infinitely replicable by governments, it is potentially subject to Gresham's Law.)

Paper currency without any gold or silver backing was rarely issued in the past. When it was, people usually avoided it, or demanded more and more of it for any good, or eventually rejected it entirely. In many people's mind, it was no different, or perhaps worse than, a clipped gold coin, even if supported by legal tender laws.

The founders of the US all opposed the creation of unbacked paper money, also known as fiat money. Alexander Hamilton, the founder of the US financial system, specifically warned against creating it, because government would inevitably issue too much of it, which he expected to lead first to "bubble" and then to crash....[44]

Today paper money (in all its variety of forms, most of which no longer involve paper) is widely accepted, but remains by definition vulnerable to rejection by consumers, precisely because it is primarily backed by consumer confidence. Legal tender laws requiring the seller to accept it also provide support, but these laws would collapse if consumers lost confidence.

75. Corollary D of Law of Money: "Paper" Money and Inflation (Anyone holding paper money while prices are rising is constantly suffering some degree of debasement.)

Rising prices mean that paper money is always being debased, either gradually or rapidly depending on the rate of inflation. For the first 125 years of American history, consumer prices rose and fell, sometimes dramatically during and after wars, but ended up about where they started. Since the establishment of the US Federal Reserve Bank in 1914, the purchasing power of the dollar has fallen by 97%, based on official government reports, which may actually understate consumer price increases, as we shall discuss below.

Americans lost almost all the purchasing power of their money over a century, and most of the loss occurred just in the past sixty years. Germans in the early 1920s lost 100% of the purchasing power of their cash savings in only a few years, and so have many others during the numerous great inflations of world history. Many people think that cash is a "safe" investment, but this illustrates that paper currency is anything but safe.

76. *Corollary E of Law of Money: (Law of) Diversification* (Although cash is a risky, not a riskless investment, all other investments are risky, too. Fortunately the risks are not all the same, which enables an investor to seek to control overall risk.)

Although there is no such thing as a "safe" investment, the price of one may rise with inflation, while another may rise during crashes and depressions, and so forth. The degree of protection is always unknowable, but in general owning productive assets is a better bet during an inflation than owning cash or bonds while the reverse is true during an economic crash. Consequently, only diversification of investment across a variety of investments, with different characteristics of risk and reward, particularly businesses, real properties, financial instruments such as cash or bonds, and precious metals, provides at least some degree of protection against the unknown.

Diversification based on a measurement of historic correlation of returns is inherently unreliable. For example, there have been periods when stocks and bonds have risen and fallen together and other periods in which they have done just the opposite. The underlying data point observations may also be unreliable. One must therefore choose assets for diversification based on the logic of their economic characteristics (such as resistance to inflation or deflation) rather than on naïve extrapolation of financial history.

77. *Corollary F of Law of Money: (Law of) Investment Value*: (Another important way to reduce risk is to avoid investments that have recently become more expensive without a clear change in earning power or that are currently winning a "popularity" contest.)

If two companies are of equal quality, the one with the lower share price offers less risk and more reward by definition. Of course no two companies are ever identical, so it is primarily a matter of judgment.

In addition, the near-term result will be moved as much by market mood as by price fundamentals. If the mood of the market is optimistic and speculative, cheap is likely to become cheaper, because the market is less concerned with price and therefore likely to ignore a bargain. Expensive is likely to become more expensive, because everyone loves a winner. If the mood shifts, and investors become more risk-averse, there is greater likelihood that this will reverse, and the cheap may become less cheap, or at least less cheap relative to the expensive.

Throughout this process, once the share has been sold by the company in an initial public offering, there will always be an owner, so long as the company does not go bankrupt. What determines the price is degree of demand relative to supply, or in this case how eager the buyers are in relation to the sellers.

All these complications aside, the higher the price of the security you buy, the less room for appreciation there is over the long run. Whatever happens in the short term, there is no more powerful determinant of risk and eventual return than the initial price paid.

Chapter XIII

Laws of Money Prices

78. *Law of Money Prices*: It is an error to think of money as inherently different from other products and services; it too is subject to supply and demand.

I F THE SUPPLY of money goes up, all else being equal, the price of money expressed in other goods would be expected to fall. If the supply goes down, the price would be expected to rise.

We do not, however, typically think in these terms, that is, we do not think in terms of the price of money itself. We find it more useful and less confusing to think of the price of goods and services expressed in money. Consequently when we speak of the price of an automobile, that price will actually reflect three factors: supply of the product, which summarizes a great variety of underlying fundamental factors and trends; demand for the product, which also summarizes underlying fundamental factors and trends; and the supply/demand for money itself. No wonder people, even economists, become confused by all these interactions.

79. *Corollary A of Law of Money Prices: Stabilizing Prices* (Attempts to stabilize money prices will just destabilize the economic system.)

This follows both from Corollary G of the Law of Analytic Laws (Law of Unintended Consequences) and from the law of prices in general.

Here is an example of someone arguing in favor of attempting to stabilize prices, taken from this author's book *Are The Rich Necessary?*:

> When we order flour or sugar, we expect to get a specified weight in pounds or kilograms. When we travel from city to city, we also know that we can rely on standard units of measurement, whether miles or kilometers. Imagine, now, that pounds, kilograms, miles, and kilometers all fluctuated in value from day to day. Economic chaos would ensue.
>
> If we do not accept fluctuating weights and distances, why should we accept fluctuating

money values? Not knowing what a dollar or euro will be worth tomorrow, expressed against each other, or even more importantly expressed as an underlying basket of goods that each will buy, is confusing and disorienting.[45]

This is a popular argument, one articulated by Steve Forbes, publisher of *Forbes Magazine*, and many others. It may sound reasonable at first glance, but does not hold up on closer inspection. *New Yorker* writer Adam Gopnik goes even further, suggesting that unequal incomes are equivalent to corrupted legal measurements: "A society with gross inequities of measure, whether of inches or of incomes, cannot sustain itself."[46]

The problem with these ideas is that money prices have nothing in common with weights and distances. Nor should we want them to be stable. The law of prices reminds us that money prices, including wages, represent a discovery and information system. They "discover" and inform producers and consumers about how changes in the demand and supply for goods and services are currently interacting with changes in the demand and supply for money to create our latest money prices.

These changing prices are ultimately guided by consumer preferences. They tell us what consumers want now, when and where they want it, and what price they are willing to pay for it. This is not perfect or complete information. But it is just enough and good enough information to enable producers to make rational decisions about their investments and production.

Any attempt on the part of government to stabilize or fix money prices will interrupt and damage this information flow. Whatever the intentions are, it can only backfire. It is rather like poking a stick into the wheels of a tire. The tire may be more "stable," but the car does not move.

We can state that a foot is twelve inches or a meter one hundred centimeters because we are defining our own terms. But if we understand the role of prices, we understand that they are meant to be in flux, and trying to pin them down will harm, not help, the economy. The reality, in economist Wilhelm Röpke's words, is that "The more [government] stabilization, the less stability."[47]

80. *Corollary B of Law of Money Prices: Measuring Prices* (Attempts to stabilize money prices also presume that we can reliably measure economy-wide prices, which is false.)

Yes, we can estimate what an apple of a particular kind and quality costs at a particular time and location. But the attempt to measure prices as a whole across the entire economy is a classic will o' the wisp.

Economists have sought to accomplish this by creating price indexes, which are defined as "shopping baskets" of goods and services weighted in some specified way and followed over time. Unfortunately both the methods and the results are inherently arbitrary. And they have been made even more arbitrary by obscure methodological changes made for what appear to be political purposes.

In the US, changes made by the Clinton administration seemed especially suspicious, in that they tended to reduce reported inflation, and this was politically very useful. In the first place, it reduced government Social Security program payments, which President Reagan had linked to inflation indexes in order to rein in government's proclivity to inflate prices, about which, more below. It also made the Clinton administration look more successful in the economic record, since every point reduction in reported inflation increases reported "real" economic growth.

A shrewd observation by social psychologist Donald T. Campbell in 1976 about this kind of phenomenon is sometimes called "Campbell's Law":

> The more any quantitative social indicator is used for social decision-making, the more subject it will be to corruption pressures and the more apt it will be to distort and corrupt the social processes it is intended to monitor.[48]

Campbell's Law is also related to the Goodhart Law (Charles Goodhart, 1975): Once a rule is developed based on social data, the data will be gamed); and the

Lucas Critique (Robert Lucas, 1976): It is naïve to rely on so-called empirical social data series to guide our policy making. It also relates to Corollary F of the Law of Analytic Laws discussed earlier.

81. *Corollary C of Law of Money Prices: "Elastic" Money Supply* (Another fallacy that is economically destructive.)

If you believe that government should keep prices as stable as possible, then you must also believe that the amount of money in the economy must be "elastic." Think of it this way. If we have only four apples and four dollars, each apple might be expected to be priced at a dollar. If you double the number of apples to eight, the likely price would fall to 50 cents, all else remaining unchanged. This change represents unstable prices, so would be unacceptable to the money price stabilizers.

Government could "solve" this "instability" by creating and distributing four more dollars. Now the apples are again sold for a dollar. In economic jargon, the money supply has become "elastic." But what has been gained? Why would we want apples to cost more? Will not lower prices help everyone, the poor and middle class in particular?

Supporters of the Federal Reserve Act of 1913 loudly demanded "elastic" money on grounds that economic growth was allegedly being "thwarted," "parched," or "choked off" by a scarcity of cash in the economy. A century later, after mountains of new money had been created by the Fed and the dollar had lost most of its purchasing power, this fallacious idea still held a firm grip on popular opinion.

The truth is that there cannot be a "shortage" of money. Money may be a commodity, but money prices by definition are a discovery and communication tool. In the above example, when we had four apples and four dollars, and each apple cost a dollar, the production of four more apples made us richer, and this was communicated by the fall in apple prices.

If we had started out with four apples but only one dollar, then the starting prices would have been 25 cents and the addition of four more apples might have driven the price of each apple down to 12.5 cents. In this simple economy, why would anyone care whether the starting price of the apple is one dollar or 25 cents? What really matters is how many apples we have. This is the only factor that determines our wealth, not the number of beginning or ending dollars.

As previously noted, it is not money that makes us rich or poor. It is production. And in a real-life economy, with all its complexity, prices must not only discover and communicate. They must also balance in a way that sums up to a profit for producers. If they do not, production will be adversely affected or even collapse.

In real life, apples do not just appear. We must plant trees, tend to them, harvest, store, transport, and sell. If the cost of all this is greater than the end price, apples will likely disappear.

The specific amount of money we use to denominate our apple production is only important because it is part of a web of interrelated prices that must balance. It is not in itself important whether the total supply of apples divided by the total amount of money available to buy apples produces an apple price of $1, fifty cents, or 12.5 cents. So long as all the prices balance, the producers earn a profit, and consumers have the money to buy the product. In this case, the system is working, whatever the clearing prices are.

No specific amount of money in an economy is needed to make it work. If production increases while the money supply does not, it just means that product prices will fall. So long as our personal income does not fall, this is a positive development. We are richer.

A constant money supply is not a problem; it is an economic blessing.

82. Corollary D of Law of Money Prices: Real Wealth (It is not a matter of money.)

This has already been briefly stated under the law of money, but is worth re-emphasizing here, because people continually confuse the money price of what they own with genuine wealth. The two are not the same. Assume I hold $100. Next year I hold $110. But meanwhile the money price of what I want to buy has leapt ahead, not by 10%, but by 20%. In that case, I have more money but am poorer, not wealthier. Ultimately what we exchange with each other are real goods. If we own more real goods, we are wealthier; if we own fewer, we are poorer. Money prices are like the ancient Greek philosopher Plato's metaphor of the shadow in the cave. It is easy to confuse the shadow with the reality.

83. Corollary E of Law of Money Prices: Deflation (We should welcome it.)

This is also already implicit in previous corollaries. Although it is ultimately impossible and in the meantime counter-productive for government to try to control or manipulate money prices, this does not mean that we should be indifferent to the direction they are taking. Within particular industries, all prices must continually adjust themselves to create profits and thereby support employment. Some production prices (which we call costs) are heading up, some down, as needed to comply with current consumer demand. But for an economy as a whole, we should clearly hope that consumer prices will generally decline. The usual term for this today is deflation. We should therefore be hoping for deflation.

In the past, deflation referred not to prices, but to the amount of money in the economy. This terminology change is unfortunate because it leaves us without a simple word to describe a falling supply of money. In addition, in more recent years, deflation has begun to mean an unexpected, rapid, or violent decline in prices, as may happen in a depression. This further change creates even more confusion, because a steady, gentle, year-by-year fall in prices has little in common with a rapid or violent fall. Why use the same term to describe both one and the other?

The main point to consider is that gently falling prices both signal economic progress and benefit all consumers, especially those with less money; they should therefore be our economic goal. By contrast, rapidly falling prices represent economic failure, not success. They signal that price relationships in the economy are out of balance and need to be adjusted in order to restore profitability. This will in turn protect jobs which will also protect the consumer incomes needed to buy the products.

Left alone, producers will do what needs to be done to restore balance, because they want to survive and prosper. If they do not get costs (production prices) in line with consumer prices, they will sooner or later go bankrupt. These are powerful incentives, both positive and negative, to fix what needs fixing.

Interpreted in this light, even rapidly falling prices are not necessarily negative. Although they signal economic failure, they also indicate that the system is trying to correct itself. If prices are allowed to do their work of informing everyone what is happening at a given time, and if wages are allowed to adjust to consumer prices, there is every reason to think that the economy will rapidly right itself and both prices and employment will soon recover.

Economist John Maynard Keynes argued during the Great Depression that the system during a contraction of this magnitude would not be able to right itself, that it would just spiral endlessly downward. Keynes's brilliant disciple Franco Modigliani soon corrected this fallacy in an economic review article published in 1944, two years before his mentor's death in 1946.[49] Modigliani concluded that all the symptoms of depression, from lack of investment to deep unemployment, were caused by unbalanced prices, and that profit-seeking businesses would naturally succeed in rebalancing them.

No one has ever refuted Modigliani, because the logic is irrefutable. Economies plagued by price imbalances will naturally try to balance themselves, and will often succeed quickly. The classic example of how this should work was the Depression of 1921. It was deep but over in hardly more than a year.

Despite this, President Obama in 2009 repeated Keynes's fallacy that economic producers and consumers could not fix an economy on their own, that it could only be done by massive government intervention, that without government stimulus "crisis" would turn into "catastrophe," at which point it might be too late to "reverse." This was complete nonsense,

but Obama must have been instructed in these soph-
istries by his own economists.[50]

84. Corollary F of Law of Money Prices: Inflation (Roots of)

If deflation should be our goal, preferably gentle, steady,
year by year deflation, then why have we instead gotten
so much inflation? Why has the purchasing power of
the dollar fallen 97% since the creation of the Fed using
the government's own price index numbers, which
arguably under-report the inflation, especially in recent
decades? A passage from this author's *Are The Rich Necessary?* also explored this question:

> One popular idea is that prices rise because
> business owners are "greedy." A variant of
> this idea is the *oligopolistic* theory of infla-
> tion: "greedy" business owners band to-
> gether into cartels so that we have to accept
> their inflated prices. Alternatively, business
> owners may blame "greedy" unions for de-
> manding excessively high wages. Both busi-
> ness owners and unions may in turn blame
> "greedy" oil producers for cartelizing and
> raising global oil prices.
>
> However, . . . greed alone cannot raise prices.
> Prices only rise if demand increases because
> of a change in consumer preferences, supply

shrinks, or the supply of money used in transactions increases, and greed per se cannot affect any of these things.

Assuming that available money remains the same, price increases devised by "greedy" business owners, unions, or global oil producers will just lead to falling sales. The falling sales will lead to lower profits and employment, and lower profits and employment to lower prices and wages again. It is only when government "accommodates" rising prices by legally protecting monopolies or by "printing" and circulating more money that the higher prices can "stick" and result in inflation.

Another common and closely related idea about inflation is that it is caused by economic *overheating*, that is, by a too rapid increase in economic growth. In particular, it is assumed that such growth will lead either to production bottlenecks (in which producers' goods become scarce and expensive) or to escalating labor wage demands.

This logic is faulty. Economic growth as a whole does not decrease society's supply of goods. On the contrary, it increases the supply of goods. And we know that an increase in the supply of goods should reduce rather than increase prices.

Here again, the answer to our conundrum lies in the supply of money. If the supply of money remains constant, bottlenecks and wage demands may increase some prices, and these price increases may in turn slow the overall rate of growth. But nothing should show up in the general price level. It is only if additional dollars are created and injected by government, in an amount exceeding the increase in production, that general inflation should arise. . . .

Yet another explanation of inflation suggests that it is caused by . . . government intervening in certain industries, notably healthcare, education, and housing, to ensure that everyone has access to these critical products and services. The initial method of intervention is to provide financial subsidies. Because these subsidies tend to increase demand without increasing supply, prices rise, so that access is actually restricted rather than improved.

These problems then lead to government controls. But controls typically shrink supply even more, in addition to causing inefficiencies. [We have previously mentioned this phenomenon in the context of the eighteenth-century French price controls on wheat that contributed to mass starvation and hastened the Revolution.] Also, because markets are hobbled, innovation is thwarted, which inflates prices further, all of which leads to more demands for government to "do something," which leads to more price controls.

As prices in the quasi-public sectors of the economy keep growing, these sectors consume more and more of the consumer's paycheck. Consequently, it becomes increasingly difficult for the efficient private sector, with its steady price decreases, to bring down the overall consumer price indexes.

Expressed in terms of a three-factor model of inflation (demand, supply, and supply of money), the case is rather simple. Demand for something like healthcare is potentially infinite. Supply, however, is limited. Markets would normally sort this out by identifying a price that channeled demand to match supply while balancing supply with other pressing consumer needs and demand.

Government intervention is intended to help those who cannot pay the market price, but changes neither potentially infinite demand nor limited supply. It simply introduces more money into the equation and thus raises prices. If government paid for its subsidy by raising taxes, demand would be reduced elsewhere in the economy, so that overall prices should not rise. If the subsidy is instead covered by creating and injecting more dollars, overall prices will likely rise.

Based on the above, it is easy to see why economist Milton Friedman famously said that, "Inflation is always and everywhere a monetary phenomenon."[51] And added that:

> Just as an excessive increase in the quantity of money is the one and only important cause of inflation, so a reduction in the rate of monetary growth is the one and only cure for inflation.[52]

These statements are accurate but incomplete and therefore potentially misleading. As noted, inflation may come from any of three sources: demand, supply, or government-engineered money supply changes. [At the same time, we should note that it is not any easier to measure the quantity of money in an economy than it is to measure economy-wide price changes. Logic suggests that any government creation of new money will change prices, either of consumer goods or investment assets or both, and thereby potentially disturb the price signaling system. But we cannot calculate with precision any of this even after the fact, much less before the new money is introduced. Friedman was wrong in thinking that this could be done.]

In addition, we must also keep in mind, as noted in a prior section, that a change in the quantity of money, as important as it may be, is really less important than people's expectations about where the quantity of money is headed. In an extreme case, if people think that the government is going to run its money "printing press" faster and faster, they will try to convert their cash into tangible assets or goods, thereby changing the demand mix of the economy and ensuring that tangible asset and goods prices will rise even faster than the quantity of money.

In this sense, the quality of money, or at least perceptions about quality, count for as much or more than quantity, which is why inflation

> rates during the German Great Inflation of
> the 1920s ultimately outstripped the actual
> rate of currency printed, even with the print-
> ing presses going full throttle. . . ."[53]

This is yet another example of the law stated above under economic calculation that in economics (or any other social decision-making field), quality is even more critical than quantity in determining outcomes. Alexander the Great faced the Persian Empire with far fewer troops than his adversary, but won every battle, and this pattern repeats itself throughout the history of organized human action.

The most famous description of inflation as a monetary phenomenon was written by economist John Maynard Keynes, when still a young man, before he changed his mind and became an advocate of inflationary policies:

> Lenin is said to have declared that the best
> way to destroy the Capitalist System was
> to debauch the currency. By a continuing
> progress of inflation, governments can con-
> fiscate, secretly and unobserved, an impor-
> tant part of the wealth of their citizens. By
> this method they not only confiscate, but
> they confiscate *arbitrarily*; and while the
> process impoverishes many, it actually en-
> riches some. . . . Lenin was certainly right.

There is no subtler, no surer means of over-
turning the existing basis of society than to
debauch the currency. . . . "[54]

The youthful Keynes was right. The public at least
initially does not understand what is driving the rise
in prices. But when they do figure it out, they may
then reject the currency, with catastrophic results for
the economy.

Chapter XIV

Law of Interest Rates

85. *Law of Interest Rates (on Money Loans)*: **Lending rates reflect an inescapable social reality: that money in hand is worth more than money in the future. They also represent some of the most important prices in the economy and as such both reflect and balance supply and demand. If we interfere with them, we will lose both the vital signal and balancing services they provide. We will not improve our economic prospects.**

IF WE BORROW, we pay interest to lenders because money available in future years is worth less than money available now. If it is a good or service rather than money, this might not be true. Even squirrels appreciate that a nut is more valuable in winter than in summer. But money is always more valuable to us now, mostly because we can put it to use immediately, but also because future payments will always be uncertain to some degree, and future purchasing power will be uncertain as well. The longer the period of the loan, the more these uncertainties are magnified, which requires a higher rate of interest in compensation.

The rational preference for money now, not later, is a fact of life. Young children offered a choice of one apple now or two tomorrow commonly take the one apple now. Adults may think differently because two apples rather than one with a relatively short wait represents a high rate of reward. As noted earlier, in exchange transactions involving the transfer of money, the lender, who holds a surplus of cash, values the cash plus interest more highly than the cash alone, while the borrower values the immediate cash more, which leads to the exchange between them.

These are inescapable social realities. Government policies intended to fix the rate of interest at ever lower levels, or even flipping them entirely, so that the lender must pay the borrower, subvert the natural state of affairs between human beings and therefore cannot be sustained indefinitely. While they last, however, they distort some of the most important prices in the economy. We lose all the discovery, information, and balancing services of these prices. In addition, artificially low interest rates may temporarily increase the supply of money and thereby fuel inflation, as we shall discuss shortly.

Chapter XV

Laws of Banking

86. *Law of Banking*: **The way banking is currently set up guarantees its instability.**

ONSIDER THE RATHER curious way in which banks operate. If depositors decide to withdraw all their money at the same time, we have what is called a "*run*" on the bank, and the bank may fail. In some sense, therefore, all banks are technically "insolvent" all the time, because they never keep enough money in their vaults to meet their promise to repay depositors on demand.

Building an economy on a foundation of banks that are in some sense "insolvent" all the time is clearly a chancy undertaking. This problem was recognized as soon as gold depositories began to evolve into modern lending institutions. The question was what, if anything, would be done about it.

An effort to require banks to maintain 100% reserves against all deposits failed in British courts in 1811 and 1816 and again in the House of Lords in 1848.[55] Plaintiffs charged that the system was fraudulent, since banks keeping "fractional reserves" knew they were making promises they could not keep.

If the courts had decided differently, modern banks would operate on entirely different lines. In addition to acting as a depository, they might lend their owners' capital, act as agents for depositors' capital, or offer absolutely fixed time deposits (so that the depositor's repayment date could be matched with a borrower's repayment date).

The technical "insolvency" of banks mattered enormously in the Great Depression of the 1930s, when bank runs proliferated, and the entire banking system was temporarily shut down by the Roosevelt administration. It is usually argued that government deposit insurance has solved the problem. But the government can only make bank deposits good by creating vast sums of new money, which would then dilute the purchasing of existing money, including the deposits. So it may be argued that the government guarantee is fraudulent too.

87. *Corollary A of Law of Banking: Fractional Reserves Create Money* (We have more or less inadvertently given banks the power to create new money more or less surreptitiously.)

In addition to the threat of runs, fractional reserve banking introduces yet another element of potential instability into the economic system. Bank lending far beyond reserves through checkbook accounts is also creating what functions as new money.

To illustrate how this works, let us assume that a depositor puts $1,000 into a bank. The bank keeps $100 as a reserve and lends $900. Because the depositor still has $1,000, and the borrower now has $900, the amount of money in the economy has increased from $1,000 to $1,900.

The borrower may then use the new money to pay other people who also deposit it in their banks. The original $1,000 deposit may thus move from bank to bank and, assuming a 10% reserve requirement, keep ballooning until it has increased to $10,000.

This is not, however, a new Gospel parable of the fishes and loaves. As the money increases, so do people's debts. It is debt, not new wealth, that is being created. So long as new money and debt are being created in this way, it will have a "feel good" effect for the economy. But if it goes too far, it will become an unsustainable "bubble," and bubbles tend to pop and lead to crashes, ending in depression and unemployment.

88. *Corollary B of Law of Banking: The Federal Reserve* (The power of banks to create money has led to a government takeover of them, which is used for government's own surreptitious purposes.)

When the Federal Reserve was established in 1914, one of its first acts was to reduce required bank reserves. By doing so, it deliberately made the banking system, and ultimately the economic system as a whole, less, not more stable. Thereafter it continued to lower or raise reserves over the years, but mostly lowered them.

During the 1920s, Fed officials also discovered that they could accelerate bank new money creation through a system called "open market operations." All the Fed had to do was write one of its own checks (drawn against nothing and therefore creating new money) to purchase a government bond from a bank. The newly created cash (dubbed "high powered money") would go directly to the bank's account where it could be multiplied many fold by lending.

Best of all, this could all be done in complete privacy. Not even Congress would have a clue about what was happening behind the Fed's closed doors. The Fed even paid for its own budget by creating new money, in direct violation of the Constitution's requirement for Congressional approval of any spending.

The Fed could also reverse itself by selling government bonds to banks, but the primary goal was to "stimulate" the economy by increasing the country's money supply through lending. By giving what the head of the New York Fed called a "coup de whiskey" to the economy in the late twenties, this new technique helped to create the bubble that ended so dramatically in the 1929 Crash, leaving in its wake the Great Depression.

Open Market Operations and other techniques over the years have sometimes had the stated object of pouring large amounts of new money into the economy, sometimes the reduction of lending rates by increasing lendable funds. The two aims are so closely connected that it is difficult to distinguish between them, but interest rates are generally more measurable than money supply.

89. Corollary C of Law of Banking: Fed as Price Fixer (Everything the Fed does represents an effort to fix some of our most important economy-wide prices.)

Governments and central banks always claim that they are resorting to these methods in order to improve economic performance and thereby increase jobs. What they fail to mention is that they are also designed to get the government through the next election, to reduce the rate of interest paid by the government when it borrows, and to reduce the burden of government debt over time by inflating away the purchasing power of what is owed to bondholders.

Economist John Maynard Keynes was particularly keen on central banks driving interest rates down and keeping them there indefinitely as a way of "stimulating" economic activity. In presenting his own economic analysis, he failed to acknowledge that Fed interest rate manipulations and controls, along with related currency manipulations and controls including devaluations, are themselves price controls. This is an essential point. We have already discussed how deeply injurious price controls can be. No controlled price can do what prices are supposed to do, that is, discover and inform market participants about current economic activity.

How can we expect to help ourselves by fixing one of the most important prices in the economy, the cost of credit, which itself reflects the cost of waiting, a cost that pervades everything we do. The price of both loans and of currencies are "big" prices that pervade the entire economy. Fixing what we most need to be flexible cannot help anybody, not even government spenders. It will just produce economic bubbles that inevitably end in tears.

Just as all these price manipulations and controls destroyed the French monarchy and aristocracy in the eighteenth century, they could just as easily destroy today's global economic establishment. The reason would be the same: too many unforced economic errors, caused by disregarding the logic of economic law, fuel economic corruption and ultimately take a horrendous toll on the lives of the poor and the middle class. The intricacies of this are discussed in more detail in *Where Keynes Went Wrong*.

90. *Corollary D of Law of Banking: Reform* (Banking can be put on a more solid foundation, most obviously by eliminating fractional reserve banking.)

In order to eliminate debt money pyramid schemes, with all the tragic instability they bring to the economy, the first step would be to eliminate fractional reserve banking. The second would be to abolish the Fed. In this context, we must remember that the American economy thrived without a central bank for nearly a century and even Paul Volcker, arguably the most successful Fed Chairman, has acknowledged that inflation was better controlled without one. The third step would be to reform a world monetary system currently run by central banks.

The concept of requiring a 100% lending reserve is not as radical as it might initially appear. Arguments in its favor have been made over the years by eminent economists such as Frank Knight and Henry Simons of the University of Chicago, Irving Fisher of Yale, and in particular "Austrian" school economists led by Ludwig von Mises. Martin Wolf, the former World Bank economist and columnist for the *Financial Times*, has written: "There is [a] way of making finance safe. . . . It [is] radical: deposits would be 100% reserve backed. . . ."[56] One of the curious features of this proposal is that it has been embraced by serious thinkers on all sides of the usual political spectrum, including "socialists" and "progressives" as well as "libertarians."

Eliminating fractional reserve banking would go far toward ending the cycles of bubble and bust in the world economy. But to put economies on a completely sound financial footing, it would also be important to provide a stable and sustainable world monetary system. The world had such a system in the late nineteenth-century gold standard, but it suffered a fatal flaw. Because it was controlled by governments, it could be subverted, as it was at the onset of World War I, and then finally abandoned in its entirety, as it was in 1971.

91. *Corollary E of Law of Banking: Bank Privatization* (Money and banking services are not inherently different from other commercial services.)

Over the decades and especially since 2008, banks have been gradually nationalized. They remain nominally private, with their own shareholders and bondholders. In reality, however, they have become tightly controlled, albeit arguably overpaid, departments of government.

Because the prices of all goods and services and all economic calculations are expressed in money terms, we may fall into the error of thinking that money and banking services are different from other products and services, and that this justifies the present system of running them as virtual departments of government. But this is a misunderstanding. Both money and banking services could be provided by truly private businesses, just like other services. Good laws and genuine competition, uncorrupted by crony capitalism, could regulate them, just as they do other businesses.

There are already some glimpses of how this might work. For example, the government of Singapore allows checking accounts and debit cards denominated, not in a government-controlled currency, but in gold or silver. If more of this were allowed, entrepreneurs would innovate and find new and better ways of providing both money and banking. And we would not have to suffer the continual cronyism and crises that government control brings.

Chapter XVI

Laws of Government-Controlled Banking

92. *Law of Government-Controlled Banking*: If we allow government to continue to tighten its control of banking, we should not be surprised if government uses this control for its own purposes, not to improve prospects for the economy.

T HE PRIMARY FUNCTION of modern banks, as viewed by government, and therefore as viewed by the bankers themselves, is to help keep public sector interest rates low, to buy government bonds, and otherwise to facilitate an immense government debt, money creation, and spending operation. If you are not a government, a ward of government, allied with government, or playing a role in financing government, you should not expect the bank to pay much attention to you.

As previously noted, government control of banks and Wall Street has been kept as furtive as possible. After the Crash of 2008, the Federal Reserve could not hide that it was massively subsidizing Wall Street in order to rescue it from its own folly. But it certainly did not want to acknowledge publicly why it was doing so, which was sheer panic at the prospect of a precipitous collapse of the massive government debt operation.

The press and public were told that it was necessary to bail out Wall Street in order to protect the "Main Street" economy, but this was for cosmetic purposes. It helped that the president and many members of Congress, as well as much of the public, lacked the financial expertise to grasp the deception.

During and after the Crash, changes were instituted that made government control of finance tighter, but also more obvious. One of them was to redefine investment firms such as Goldman Sachs as "bankers" so that they could obtain (speculate with) newly created government money borrowed directly from the Fed at giveaway rates. This was a tremendous subsidy, far bigger than Congressionally approved direct bailout "TARP" funds.

A revision of the Federal Reserve Bank Statute legalized the Fed buying mortgage bonds with its newly created money, something it had already been doing illegally on a massive scale. The "Quantitative Easing" program also made it much easier for the agency to buy back from Wall Street the bonds that the Treasury Department of the government had recently sold to Wall Street.

The new authority to buy an unlimited amount of government debt ("quantitative easing") was especially critical. It is still illegal for the Fed to buy bonds directly from the government. In addition, this would make it too obvious that the government is buying bonds from itself. No government is really "borrowing" when it creates the money to buy back its own bonds. This is just a veiled way of creating whatever money it wants to spend at that moment. Despite this, the Fed has already bought and continues to "own" more US government bonds than any other party, including the governments of Japan and China.

Phony bond transactions, in which government issues a bond and buys it right back, is just an intricate and updated version of what in the past has been called "money printing." It is no different from what eventually caused the great inflations of world history, including the infamous Great German Inflation of the early 1920s.

The Fed is more in the public spotlight than ever before but still tries to operate behind closed doors. As noted above, it pays its own expenses with newly created money, free of any need for constitutionally mandated Congressional appropriation of funds or supervision. It refuses to divulge all its payments to foreign banks. It refuses even a Congressional audit, despite having been created by Congress and serving at the pleasure of Congress.

At the same time, the Fed goes to great trouble to maintain appearances. When it creates the money to buy a bond from Wall Street that has just been sold by the government, it even takes the extraordinary step of creating additional new money in order to be able to claim to send Washington "interest payments." These phony interest payments are then duly booked as legitimate federal revenue, just like taxes, and applied to "deficit reduction."

The Dodd-Frank legislation, passed after the Crash, further shored up this crooked system by requiring banks, under penalty of law, to buy a designated quota of government bonds, with of course the tacit wink that the Fed would buy them back as needed. The stated purpose of the requirement was to make banks safer by ensuring that they always had government bonds in their capital structure, as if bank managers did not know that their very existence, not to mention their salaries and stock options, depended on serving the needs of their government bosses.

93. *Corollary A of Law of Government-Controlled Banking: Government Financing Options 101 (In the end, the public pays one way or the other.)*

Taxes are inconvenient. Imposing them runs the risk of upsetting either voters or special interest campaign contributors. Borrowing is much easier, but there is a limit to how much can actually be borrowed and repaid. It is a law of economics (and life) that debt service cannot grow faster than tax revenue without sooner or later leading to bankruptcy. Debt financing can thus eventually be even more inconvenient than taxing. Creating new money surreptitiously through the sale of phony bonds is so much easier than either taxing or borrowing legitimately with the actual intention of repaying it.

From an economic point of view, new money creation in some respects resembles taxation. Here is an example. If a government taxes 25% of all income in taxes, it can thereby command 25% of all economic goods and services. If, instead, it creates new money representing a third of all existing money, it will end up at the same place, in command of 25% of all economic goods and services.

But there is a downside. Escalating debt can only be repaid by taxation or eliminated by default. Inflation provides a slow-motion default, but debt typically grows faster than it can be eliminated in this way. Creating new money with which to buy bonds relies on methods that destroy the free price system and flood the economy with new money. Eventually the new money can destroy the monetary system and with it the economy.

This surreptitious process also frees government from even the minimal financial discipline imposed by the tax or debt system. While the party lasts, crony capitalist corruption thrives and the cronies get richer and richer. Eventually the party ends and then even the cronies lose. But by the time the cronies are crying over the loss of zeroes at the end of their net worth statements, ordinary people may be starving.

Chapter XVII

Laws of Spending
Versus Saving

94. *Law of Spending Versus Saving*: **No one is so foolish as to try to spend his or her way to wealth. We create wealth by abstaining from spending, by saving, by making wise investments, and by working hard to make the investments as productive as possible. Governments are not exempt from this reality. Whether financed by taxes, debt, or money creation, its spending does not "stimulate" an economy.**

ECONOMIST JOHN MAYNARD KEYNES liked nothing better than to overturn what he considered "copybook morality," including the traditional middle-class virtues of thrift, saving, and patient investing. He mocked novelist Charles Dickens's famous character Mr. Micawber for urging spending restraint and avoidance of debt on the young: "Jam is not jam unless it is a case of jam tomorrow and never jam today."[57] He famously warned that "In the long run, we are all dead."[58]

Although Keynes's quip cannot be disputed, even the most basic math seems to rebut the recommendation to spend more and save less. Here are a few calculations from *Where Keynes Went Wrong*:

> Assume that our incomes are growing at 3% a year, thanks to the investments we have made from our savings. If we keep spending 80% and saving 20% year after year, both the amount spent and the amount saved will double by the 25th year.
>
> Even if our only ambition is to spend more, saving and investing still makes sense, because it will give us more and more money to spend, and we will not have to wait 25 years to feel the effect. Assume that my friend and I have an identical starting income. My friend spends 100% of it. I save 20% and as a result my income grows at 3%. Within only eight years, I will have more to spend than my friend, and after that the gap will steadily grow.[59]

Keynes did not deny any of this. He himself was a prodigious saver and investor, but somehow the same math was not supposed to apply to nations. In a 1934 article in the popular American magazine *Redbook*, he wrote an article titled "Can America Spend Its Way Into Recovery?" and opened with a cheery "Why Obviously!" Unfortunately the article did not really spell out why it was obvious.

95. *Corollary A of Law of Spending Versus Saving:* *"Fiscal Stimulus"* (Also referred to as "Growth" Policy)

Political leaders since the 1930s have frequently adopted Keynes's cavalier attitude in describing their own deficit spending, not as deficit spending, borrowing or "money creation," but rather as "fiscal stimulus." President Hollande of France did this one better by simply referring to it as "growth policy" or sometimes just as "growth." And President Obama immediately echoed him in copycat style.

But even if government spending is not primarily designed to win elections or subsidize cronies, even if its sole aim is to help a chronically ailing private economy, how do we know it will actually contribute to growth? And how will all of this be affected by the source of the dollars spent?

If the dollars are taxed, money that might have been invested by the private sector is instead spent by the public sector. If so, there is no "stimulus." Yes, government will spend when a wise private investor will not. But is this necessarily a good idea? Public officials lack the knowledge, the qualifications, the procedures, and the incentives to make the best investment decisions. Everything they do will be guided by politics, as pork-laden "stimulus" bills over the years have repeatedly shown.

More often, the dollars spent by government are not taxed, but rather borrowed or just created out of thin air. But why would this stimulate any better than tax spending?

In his *General Theory*, Keynes had more room to elaborate on his recommendation of deficit spending, but continued in the same dogmatic style of his earlier *Redbook* article. The essence of his position was that if voters refused to endorse his recommendation for more borrowing and spending, then their elected government representatives should do it for them. It did not occur to him that this might sound contradictory.

Keynes also confidently asserted that each dollar or pound of government spending of any origin (taxing, borrowing, or creating new money) would multiply itself at least three or four times (note the imprecision) and as much as twelve times in dollars of economic growth.[60] Subsequent empirical studies attempting to provide evidence for this claim have had to rely on hard-to-collect, unreliable, and hard-to-interpret data, but suggest that the multiplier, if it ever exists, is less than one, and as government debt grows, eventually becomes negative. The logical foundations of Keynes's assumed multiplier are even shakier. *Where Keynes Went Wrong* reviewed some of these issues:

> A few of the contradictions of Keynes's multiplier math are as follows: The multiplier becomes infinite if savings are assumed to be invested, and no one would support the idea of an infinite multiplication.

> Even if the multiplier does not self-destruct by becoming infinite, it produces peculiar results. Henry Hazlitt shows how, by Keynesian math, his own personal spending ought to multiply by 100,000. He also shows how Keynes confuses nominal (before inflation) and real (after inflation) values.

> It is also incorrect, as economist George Reisman has pointed out, that the money would travel from one worker to another as it is multiplied. The spending of the first set of workers would actually be expected to increase the profits of businesses. Reisman also notes in his book *Capitalism* that Keynes's "multiplier" doctrine contradicts his own "marginal efficiency of capital" (read profits) doctrine. This is awkward for Keynes for two different reasons. In the first place, he does not want to acknowledge the role of profits in

creating employment. In the second place, profits are savings, and the multiplier formula assumes that savings are not spent. If savings are spent, the multiplier becomes infinite, as we have seen. If savings in the form of profits are not spent, there will be no multiplication. The best way to deal with all this is to put a quantified and forecastable money multiplier where it belongs: in the dustbin.[61]

Boiled down to its essence, the doctrine of "stimulus" spending would have us believe that there can never be too much spending or debt. If the economy is choking on bad debt, much of it caused or encouraged by deficit spending, the solution is to add more. The quality of spending and investment is irrelevant. Keynes jokes that if we cannot think of anything else to spend money on, just build more pyramids or bury banknotes that the private sector can go to work digging up. Just as new money is just as "genuine" as real savings, economic bubble profits are just as good as real profits, and prices set by experts like Keynes are just as good as real prices.

President Obama got into the spirit of this paradoxicalism in his first budget message titled "A New Era of Responsibility." He claimed that the increased borrowing and spending in his budget would lead the country away from a culture of "instant gratification" and toward one of "saving and investment." He added that, in order to bring healthcare costs down, it would be necessary to increase government spending on healthcare.[62]

Eighteenth-century philosopher and economist David Hume warned us about all this long ago:

> Our modern expedient, which has become very general, is to mortgage the public revenues, and to trust that posterity will pay off the encumbrances contracted by their ancestors: . . . [This is] . . . a . . . ruinous . . . practice. . . . Mankind are, in all ages, caught by the same baits: the same tricks played over and over again. . . .[63]

96. Corollary B of Law of Spending Versus Saving: Keynesian Financing "Tricks" (Borrowing is cheaper but more destructive if interest rates are controlled and especially if government borrows from itself.)

Keynes himself referred to his policy recommendations as "tricks."[64] He also labeled the large amounts of new money he wanted to create "green cheese,"[65] which echoed the old English saying that if you are foolish enough to believe in something, it means you would also believe the moon is made of green cheese. It cannot be said that Keynes lacked a sense of humor.

The Keynesian recommendation to keep doubling down on borrowing and spending is of course closely linked to the recommendation to create more and more new money in order to drive down interest rates, which in turn facilitates borrowing and spending, both by the private and the public sector. If this is causing a pileup of bad debt, just drive rates down even further in order to make it easier to repay the bad debt and to encourage new debt to layer on top of the old bad debt. As we have seen earlier, government can take advantage of the low rates in two ways: by borrowing from lenders with at least a promise to repay or by borrowing from the lenders and then buying the loans right back with newly created money.

Keynes also rather startlingly asserted that money newly created by government was equivalent to savings (his actual words were "just as genuine as any other savings)."[66] Since he was simultaneously insisting that economies at the time were plagued by too much saving, his recommendation to pour in large sums of additional "genuine savings" in the form of newly created money did seem to defy both ordinary language and common sense.

The Orwellian claim that newly created money is equivalent to "genuine savings" has never been endorsed by any of Keynes's followers—and for good reason. In the first place, savings, unlike new money, do not change the ratio of money to goods, and are therefore not inflationary. In the second place, newly created money, insofar as it at least temporarily drives down interest rates, tends to thwart or even destroy the act of saving.

Keynes responded that low interest rates actually encouraged savings because they produced more income to be saved, but this was circular and specious reasoning. Federal Reserve of Atlanta president Malcolm Bryant was more honest when he stated in 1957 that:

> If a [government] policy of active or permissive inflation is to be a fact . . . we should have the decency to say to the money saver, "Hold still, Little Fish! All we intend to do is to gut you."[67]

Although Keynes wanted to drive interest rates eventually to zero,[68] and keep them there, which would also seem to defy common sense, his followers have taken this one step further by recommending negative interest rates. Negative rates turn economic logic completely on its head by requiring lenders to pay borrowers, and have been widely implemented by central banks, especially in Japan and Europe. The monetary planners in charge find various rationalizations for explaining how they expect a system based on profit to survive such follies.

None of this makes any sense. As economist Friedrich Hayek said in the 1930s:

> To combat the depression by [printing more money and encouraging more debt] is to attempt to cure the evil by the very means which brought it about.[69]

All such attempts are equivalent to trying to cure a hangover with alcohol. They defy logic because they defy reality.

Keynes also told us that "the power of vested interests is vastly exaggerated compared to the gradual encroachment of ideas."[70] This too he turned on its head by developing ideas conveniently supportive of vested interests, and especially supportive of public leaders wishing to avoid an inconvenient choice between less spending and more taxes. Deficit finance for "stimulus," well lubricated by creating massive amounts of new money, enabled public officials to escape this dilemma entirely, at least for the time they would be in office.

Chapter XVIII

Law of the Non-Neutrality of Money

97. *Law of the Non-Neutrality of Money*: Injecting new money into the economy from any source, whether fractional reserve banking, "quantitative easing," or "fiscal stimulus," by definition cannot be neutral, contrary to assertions in most economic textbooks. Non-neutrality of money matters a great deal for an economy.

EIGHTEENTH-CENTURY PHILOSOPHER and economist David Hume explained that new money cannot and does not reach everyone at the same moment or in the same amount, and therefore cannot be economically neutral in its impact. He wrote that:

> We fancy, because an individual would be much richer, were his stock of money doubled, that the same good effect would follow, were the money of every one increased; not considering that this would raise as much the price of every commodity, and reduce every man in time to the same condition as before. . . .[71] [But] . . . time is required before the money circulates through the whole state, and makes its effect be felt on all ranks of people. At first, no alteration is perceived; by degrees the price rises, first of one commodity, then of another. . . .[72]

Here is an example of what Hume is describing. Imagine that government engages in "fiscal stimulus" by spending newly created money to pay contractors to do some work. These contractors receive the new money first. This is a windfall for them. Their income has just gone up, but the prices of what they must buy, including the labor of their own employees, has not yet gone up.

For a time, these contractors have new purchasing power that no one else has. As they begin to make purchases themselves, the new money will begin to travel elsewhere in the economy, but no one can predict exactly where it will go and how long it will take. As the money flows, it will likely increase prices elsewhere. Some people will benefit from these higher prices, others will be made poorer by them. The unluckiest will never see any increase in their income from the new money while having to pay higher prices for their consumer goods.

This is not a fair process. But, worse, it is an excellent way to confuse and disorient the price system. The more new money comes into the economy in this way, the harder will it be for prices to do what they are supposed to do, which is to discover and communicate what everyone is doing and especially what everyone wants. The dominating factor will become what the government is doing and wanting, and all the price signals will become muddled.

Most economic textbooks simply ignore all this. They assume that any new money coming into the economy reaches everyone at the same time. If that were true, it would not matter so much. To return to our earlier example, if a desert island economy consists of four knives and four dollars, so that each knife costs a dollar, and each of two people own two of the knives, it will not matter much if four more dollars wash up sealed in a bottle and are divided between the two people. Perhaps the knives will now be valued at two dollars each, but who cares?

What the government does with its economic interventions is not at all the same thing. It may be intended to serve the interests of politicians or to "stabilize" the economy. Whichever it is, the result will not be the intended consequence. It will be destabilization.

The economic textbooks, in treating money as neutral, follow economist John Maynard Keynes, but ironically the younger Keynes, before he became what today would be called a Keynesian, fully acknowledged the non-neutrality of money:

> Even if the ultimate effects of monetary effects on different prices were to be, at long last, uniform, this will be less important than the initial variability.... The fact that monetary changes do not affect all prices in the same way, in the same degree, or at the same time, is what makes them significant.[73]

The younger Keynes was right. The non-neutrality of money is a fact, a very significant fact, and one that undermines his own later monetary recommendations.

Chapter XIX

Law of the Non-Neutrality of Money, Newly Created Money, "Business Cycles," and Depressions

98. *Law of the Non-Neutrality of Money, Newly Created Money, "Business Cycles," and Depressions*: The most fundamental source of chronic economic bubble and bust.

ECONOMIC WRITER HENRY HAZLITT has explained these relationships with his usual clarity:

> [The injection of newly created money into the economy] turns out to be merely one more example of our central lesson [that

economics must focus on the long run, not just the short run, and consider all groups, not just some]. It may indeed bring benefits for a short time to favored groups, but only at the expense of others. And in the long run it brings disastrous consequences to the whole community.

Even a relatively mild [injection of new money] distorts the structure of production. It leads to the overexpansion of some industries at the expense of others. This involves a misapplication and waste of capital. When the [process of injecting money] collapses, or is brought to a halt, the misdirected capital investment—whether in the form of machines, factories, or office buildings—cannot yield an adequate return and loses the greater part of its value.

Nor is it possible to bring [the process of injecting new money] to a smooth and gentle stop, and so avert a subsequent depression.... Both political and economic forces will have got out of hand....

The value of money . . . depends upon the subjective valuations of the people who hold it. And those valuations do not depend solely on the quantity of it that each person holds. They depend also on the *quality* of the money. . . . The present valuation will often depend upon what people expect the *future* quantity of money to be. And, as with commodities on the speculative exchanges, each person's valuation of money is affected not only by what *he* thinks its value is but by what he thinks is going to be *everybody else's* valuation of money.

All this explains why, when superinflation has once set in, the value of the monetary unit drops at a far faster rate than the quantity of money either is or can be increased. When this stage is reached, the disaster is nearly complete; and the scheme is bankrupt.

Yet the ardor for [creating and injecting new money] never dies. It would almost seem as if no country is capable of profiting from the experience of another and no generation of learning from the sufferings of its forebears. Each generation and country follow the same mirage. . . . For it is the nature of [newly created money] to give birth to a thousand illusions.

In our own day the most persistent argument put forward for [injecting new money] is that it will "get the wheels of industry turning," . . .

that it . . . will bring "full employment." This argument in its cruder form rests on the immemorial confusion between money and real wealth. It assumes that new "purchasing power" is being brought into existence, and that the effects of this new purchasing power multiply themselves in ever-widening circles, like the ripples caused by a stone thrown into a pond.

The real purchasing power for goods, however, . . . consists of other goods. It cannot be wondrously increased merely by printing more pieces of paper called dollars. Fundamentally what happens in an exchange economy is that the things that A produces are exchanged for the things that B produces.

The . . . advocates of [injecting new money] . . . end by deceiving even themselves. They begin to talk of paper money, like the more naive inflationists, as if it were itself a form of wealth that could be created at will on the printing press. They even solemnly discuss a "multiplier," by which every dollar printed and spent by the government becomes magically the equivalent of several dollars added to the wealth of the country.

In brief, they divert both the public attention and their own from the real causes of a . . . depression. For the real causes, most of the time, are maladjustments within the wage-cost-price structure: maladjustments between wages and prices, between prices of raw materials and prices of finished goods, or between one price and another, or one wage and another. At some point these maladjustments have removed the incentive to produce, or have made it actually impossible for production to continue; and through the organic interdependence of our exchange economy, depression spreads. Not until these maladjustments are corrected can full production and employment be resumed. . . .

[New money] throws a veil of illusion over every economic process. [It] is the opium of the people. . . . And this is precisely its political function. It is because [new money] confuses everything that it is so consistently resorted to by our modern "planned economy" governments.

[For government to create new money to facilitate its spending] . . . is . . . a form of taxation. It is perhaps the worst possible form, which usually bears hardest on those least able to pay.... It discourages all prudence and thrift. It encourages squandering, gambling, reckless waste of all kinds. It often makes it more profitable to speculate than to produce. It tears apart the whole fabric of stable economic relationships. Its inexcusable injustices drive men toward desperate remedies. It plants the seeds of fascism and communism. It leads men to demand totalitarian controls. It ends invariably in bitter disillusion and collapse.[74]

Hazlitt's comment that reckless new money creation leads to gambling and collapse echoes what the young John Maynard Keynes had said, that it turns an economy into "a gamble and a lottery," that "it engages all the hidden forces of economic law on the side of destruction."[75] In effect, Keynes at that stage in his career, before he himself became a "Keynesian," was arguing that such policies exploited economic law for nihilist ends.

None of this is exactly new for economists. John Stuart Mill, one of the greatest nineteenth-century economists, had already written about it in 1830:

When the delusion [caused by new money] vanishes, those whose commodities are relatively in excess must diminish their production or be ruined; and if during the high prices they have built mills and erected machinery, they will be likely to repent at leisure.[76]

Contemporary monetary economists go to great lengths to avoid acknowledging the reality described by both Hazlitt and the young Keynes. Fed chairman Janet Yellen solemnly tells Congress that the Fed has failed to achieve its goal of "price stability." She does not mean that prices are heading up despite her best efforts to hold them back. On the contrary, in her Orwellian Fed speak, she is complaining that the Fed has not achieved the rising prices it actually seeks, despite its statutory mandate to keep prices stable. In this instance, as in others, if you do not like the law, in this case the statutory as well as economic law, under which you are operating, just ignore ordinary language and willfully distort the meaning of words.

Lael Brainard, a Fed governor quoted earlier, noted in a speech that Japan and Europe had not renewed economic growth by creating mountains of new money. She concluded from this, not that the policy had failed, as it had, but that the US should create even more new money. Economic writer Jim Grant forthrightly summarized the contradictory nature of what she was saying in obscure monetary jargon:

> In other words, let us emulate the interventionist policies of the Bank of Japan and the European Central Bank to ensure that America does not come to resemble Japan or France.[77]

Chapter XX

Summary Laws of Economics

99. *Summary Law of Economics*: **If you want a thriving economy, protect free and flexible prices.**

THIS FINAL LAW follows from everything that has preceded it. An economy is a trust system. It prospers to the degree that truthful prices enable us to communicate and compete with one another within an overall framework of cooperation. Both truth and trust falter or fail when prices are interfered with, manipulated, or controlled by political authorities. We then reap a whirlwind of political corruption and economic hardship.

Some of the various ways that governments interfere with prices have already been mentioned. A complete list would be too long to enumerate. A shorter list would include: direct price controls, sometimes set in collusion with special interests, price floors, supply restrictions, grants of monopoly, extensions of monopolies, restrictions through licensing, subsidies (both direct and indirect), easy or cheap credit, favors in government purchases, non-competitive bidding, bailouts, targeted tax breaks and penalties, favors in legislation or regulation, protection from new competition, protection from lawsuit or other legal threats or expenses, other ways of picking economic winners and losers, etc.

In return, public officials expect hard (illegal) or soft (legal) bribes such as campaign contributions, other campaign assistance, help "messaging," loans, "sweetheart" investment opportunities, support from "foundations," regulatory fees to substitute for general taxes, jobs for family, friends, or (eventually after leaving office) self, travel, entertainment, or other "favors," general support, and deference.

The great British statesman and historian Lord Macaulay argued that we generally survive such corruption:

> Profuse government expenditure, heavy taxation, absurd commercial restriction, corrupt tribunals, disastrous wars, . . . persecutions, conflagrations, inundations, have not been able to destroy capital so fast as the exertions of private citizens have been able to create it.[78]

Macaulay was describing recent centuries. It is true that since the late eighteenth century, private capital has grown, however slowly and fitfully, despite government corruption. Billions of us would not otherwise be alive. Before the eighteenth century and the beginning of the industrial revolution, the record shows that virtually all capital was eventually consumed, stolen, or destroyed. There were ups and downs but virtually no sustained economic growth for most of human history.

Moreover, crony capitalist corruption tends to feed on itself, especially in the modern era. The more lying, cheating, and theft there are, the more there will be. If this process runs unchecked, it can eventually lead to yet another economic and social collapse. The most reliable way to avoid this is to keep powers of government divided, as they are by the US constitution, and in addition to keep government and economy divided, so that government's sole role in the economy is to make and enforce laws for all, not to "lead" or "run" the economy itself.

100. *Corollary A of Summary Law of Economics* (The test that distinguishes good government law pertaining to the economy from bad is that good government law does not interfere with, manipulate, or control prices.)

Summary List of One Hundred Laws

Laws of Economic Analysis (Chapter I)

1. Law of Analytic Laws: If . . . then analysis assists us just as much in the social realm as in the physical realm. [See page 165.]

2. Corollary A: Material Life (If we restrict our inquiry to material life, we will misunderstand economic laws.) [See page 166.]

3. Corollary B: Boundaries (If we look for economic laws only outside ourselves, we will also misunderstand them.) [See page 167.]

4. Corollary C: Physical Science Myopia (If we only look through the lens of the physical sciences, we will also misunderstand economic and other social laws.) [See page 167.]

5. Corollary D: Logic (If we concentrate on ordinary logic, the kind of logic we use to police our everyday language, it will give us the best results in identifying, defining, and using economic laws.) [See page 169.]

6. Corollary E: Mathematics (It is an essential tool for economic calculation, but if we try to use it in the same way it is used in the physical sciences, the results will not be helpful to us.) [See page 173.]

7. Corollary F: Economic Data (Observations from the past are not relevant or reliable enough for more than limited use. If you base decisions on old correlations, you will likely make poor decisions.) [See page 174.]

8. Corollary G: Predicting the Future (In relying on economic laws, we should understand that they are usually probabilistic in nature.) [See page 177.]

9. Corollary H: Immutability (No matter how much we change, the underlying tenets of economic law do not change.) [See page 178.]

10. Corollary I: Universality (Economic laws apply without exception to everyone.) [See page 179.]

11. Corollary J: Corruption (If we rely on laws, physical or social, there will be attempts to corrupt and misuse them.) [See page 180.]

Laws of Economic Sustainability (Chapter II)

12. Law of Sustainability: Economic laws are concerned with and help guide us toward sustainability. [See page 181.]

13. Corollary A: Unintended Consequences (A refusal to think sustainably produces unintended but usually not unforeseeable negative consequences.) [See page 182.]

Laws of the Division of Labor (Chapter III)

14. Law of the Division of Labor: If we share labor, we may be able to make ourselves much more productive. [See page 185.]

15. Corollary A: Voluntary Exchange (If we emphasize not just exchange of labor, but voluntary exchange of both labor and goods, we will get better and more reliable results.) [See page 186.]

16. Corollary B: Private Ownership (If we are to exchange, we must first own.) [See page 187.]

17. Corollary C: Potential Diseconomies of Scale (If we exchange labor, it must be carefully organized, or we may become less, not more productive.) [See page 188.]

18. Corollary D: Diminishing Returns (If we add to one input without considering the effect on other inputs and the total process, we may disrupt rather than enhance production.) [See page 188.]

19. Corollary E: Potential Economies of Scale: (If we scale up in a logical way, it can make us far more productive.) [See page 189.]

20. Corollary F: Comparative Advantage or Shared Advantage (Even if different parties or countries are ill-matched in skill or resources, they will do better cooperating.) [See page 190.]

21. Corollary G: Absolute Advantage (Even if one party or country has all the skills and resources and the other has none, they are still better off cooperating.) [See page 191.]

22. Corollary H: Deceptive Trade Practices (What is called "free trade" by governments may actually be the opposite of genuine free trade and may destroy the potential benefits of a global division of labor.) [See page 193.]

23. Corollary I: Scale of Participation (If people choose not to participate in shared labor, either because they do not work at all or because they do not share their work, everyone will have less than they might have had.) [See page 195.]

Laws of Prices (Chapter IV)

24. Law of Prices: If we wish to cooperate on a voluntary basis, we must have shared, workable, flexible prices. [See page 197.]

25. Corollary A: Discovery and Communication (If shared prices are to help us, they must operate as

both a discovery and information system.) [See page 198.]

26. Corollary B: Order (If we allow prices to do their job, they will create, maintain, and enhance economic and social order.) [See page 199.]

27. Corollary C: Honest Prices (If we want prices to do their job effectively, we must refrain from manipulating, controlling, or corrupting them.) [See page 201.]

28. Corollary D: Supply (If we want to lower prices, the most effective way to do so is not to try to control them, but rather to increase supply.) [See page 203.]

29. Corollary E: Demand (If we want to increase prices, for example wages, the most effective way to do so is not to mandate it, but to increase demand.) [See page 204.]

30. Corollary F: Supply and Demand (If we allow supply and demand to operate, they will balance each other in a way that reflects consumer preferences.) [See page 204.]

31. Corollary G: One Price (Markets tend to produce a single price for a given good.) [See page 206.]

32. Corollary H: Marginal Utility (If you are trying to price your product, you cannot just take costs and add a profit margin in order to arrive at a solution. You will have to start with what the buyer will pay

at this moment for this product, anticipate correctly what the buyer will pay in the near future, and then see if you can keep production costs below this figure.) [See page 207.]

33. Corollary I: Monopoly (An attempt to thwart consumer power over prices tends to fail without government support. Although modern governments pretend to police monopoly, the policeman is easily bought off with protection money of one kind or another.) [See page 210.]

Laws of Profits (Chapter V)

34. Law of Profits: If you want lower prices for ordinary people, do not try to abolish profits. The existence of profits tends to bring prices down. [See page 213.]

35. Corollary A: Consumer Control (If you want ordinary people to control the economic system, then profits are essential for that purpose as well.) [See page 216.]

36. Corollary B: Patience (If you are unwilling to think very long term, even beyond your lifespan, you will not be able to realize the full fruits of the profit system.) [See page 216.]

37. Corollary C: "Speculation" (If you want to earn large profits, do not think that it is enough to speculate.) [See page 217.]

38. Corollary D: Loss and Bankruptcy (If you think the profit system is primarily about profit, you misread the signals it is trying to send you.) [See page 218.]

39. Corollary E: Change (If you want to earn a profit, you must embrace change.) [See page 218.]

40. Corollary F: Changing Ideas: (Often the chief barrier to economic progress, as measured by productivity, is not scarcity of capital, skilled workers, or technology, but rather the human reluctance to give up old ideas.) [See page 219.]

41. Corollary G: "Frictional" Unemployment ("Full employment" may signal an economy with a better past than future.) [See page 221.]

Laws of Profits and Wages (Chapter VI)

42. The Law of Profits and Wages: If your goal is to raise wages, the price and profit system best accomplishes that. [See page 223.]

43. Corollary A: Union Wage Gains (If the goal is to increase the share of total business revenue earned by workers, unions do not help.) [See page 224.]

44. Corollary B: Mandated Wage Floors or Gains (If the goal is to help workers, these also fail their intended purpose.) [See page 225.]

45. Corollary C: Say's Law of Supply and Demand (If you want to increase demand, logically you should start by increasing supply.) [See page 229.]

Laws of Economic Equality and Inequality (Chapter VII)

rather than of outcome, this does not in any way condone "greed.") [See page 246.]

52. Corollary D: The "Trickle Down" Fallacy (We need not fear that the success of the rich will impoverish the poor.) [See page 248.]

53. Corollary E: Wealth Taxes (If you want to help the poor or middle class, do not tax wealth.) [See page 249.]

54. Corollary F: Wealth "Redistribution" (It is not advisable, but there are better and worse ways to do it.) [See page 250.]

55. Corollary G: Making the Worker the Boss (Employee ownership as a potential way to "redistribute" income more broadly is also problematic.) [See page 253.]

Laws of the Division of Labor within the Free Price System (Chapter VIII)

56. Summary Law of the Division of Labor within the Free Price System: If we wish to be economically successful and prosperous, we must choose competition within an overall framework of cooperation, and in doing so, reject other choices, such as tribalism. [See page 255.]

57. Corollary A: Competition within an Overall System of Cooperation (This necessarily produces superior economic results relative to either competition or cooperation alone.) [See page 257.]

58. Corollary B: Growing Networks (There is no limit to the number of people who can simultaneously compete and cooperate in this way.) [See page 258.]

59. Corollary C: Worldliness Redefined (Aggression no longer pays.) [See page 259.]

60. Corollary D: Nation Size (In this new world, with respect to political units, "small is beautiful.") [See page 259.]

61. Corollary E: Individualism and Cooperatism (Contrary to common assumption, the two are actually synonymous.) [See page 260.]

62. Corollary F: World Governments Today (Not only nihilist terrorist organizations, but also national governments, especially the world's "great powers," continually threaten to pull us back into atavistic and destructive tribalism.) [See page 262.]

Laws of Economic Calculation (Chapter IX)

63. Law of Economic Calculation: If we wish to succeed economically, we must take full advantage of economic calculation. [See page 265.]

64. Corollary A: Measuring Change (As noted earlier, if the goal is economic progress, change is inescapable, and economic calculation is the essential tool to manage and promote intended rather than unintended change.) [See page 267.]

65. Corollary B: Limits of Calculation (As in everything else, it is quality of economic calculation, and attention to its limits, that matters most. Net present value offers an especially helpful perspective in that it keeps us focused on the long term, not just backward-looking financial statements.) [See page 268.]

66. Corollary C: Externalities (For society to make best use of economic calculation, we must understand this limitation in particular.) [See page 270.]

Laws of Economic Calculation outside Business (Chapter X)

67. Law of Economic Calculation outside Business: Whatever its limitations outside business, it is still the essential tool. [See page 273.]

68. Corollary A: "Borrowed Prices" (In order for a government to calculate, it must "borrow" prices.) [See page 274.]

69. Corollary B: Halfway Houses between Socialism and a Free Price System (If we mix Socialism with the Free Price System, we should not expect optimal results.) [See page 276.]

Economic Law of Government (Chapter XI)

70. Summary Economic Law of Government: The deeper government gets into controlling the economy, the more social and economic corruption it creates. [See page 279.]

Laws of Money (Chapter XII)

71. Law of Money: If people accept and use something as money without first having to convert it to money, then it is money. It is not legal tender laws that make it money. [See page 281.]

72. Corollary A: Gold (Although gold today is not "legal tender," it still functions as an "alternative" currency.) [See page 282.]

73. Corollary B: Gresham's Law (If money is debased by government, the inferior money will tend to drive good money from circulation.) [See page 283.]

74. Corollary C: "Paper" Money (Given that "paper" money has even less gold in it than a clipped or diluted coin, and as noted above is infinitely replicable by governments, it is potentially subject to Gresham's Law.) [See page 284.]

75. Corollary D: "Paper" Money and Inflation (Anyone holding paper money while prices are rising is constantly suffering some degree of debasement.) [See page 285.]

76. Corollary E: Diversification (Although cash is a risky, not a riskless investment, all other investments are risky, too. Fortunately the risks are not all the same, which enables an investor to seek to control overall risk.) [See page 286.]

77. Corollary F: Investment Value (Another important way to reduce risk is to avoid investments

that have recently become more expensive without a clear change in earning power or that are currently winning a "popularity" contest.) [See page 287.]

Laws of Money Prices (Chapter XIII)

78. Law of Money Prices: It is an error to think of money as inherently different from other products and services; it too is subject to supply and demand. [See page 289.]

79. Corollary A: Stabilizing Prices (Attempts to stabilize money prices will just destabilize the economic system.) [See page 290.]

80. Corollary B: Measuring Prices (Attempts to stabilize money prices also presume that we can reliably measure economy-wide prices, which is false.) [See page 292.]

81. Corollary C: "Elastic" Money Supply (Another fallacy that is economically destructive.) [See page 294.]

82. Corollary D: Real Wealth (It is not a matter of money.) [See page 296.]

83. Corollary E: Deflation (We should welcome it.) [See page 297.]

84. Corollary F: Inflation (Roots of) [See page 300.]

Law of Interest Rates (Chapter XIV)

85. Law of Interest Rates (on Money Loans): Lending rates reflect an inescapable social reality: that money in hand is worth more than money in the future. They also represent some of the most important prices in the economy and as such both reflect and balance supply and demand. If we interfere with them, we will lose both the vital signal and balancing services they provide. We will not improve our economic prospects. [See page 309.]

Laws of Banking (Chapter XV)

86. Law of Banking: The way banking is currently set up guarantees its instability. [See page 311.]

87. Corollary A: Fractional Reserves Create Money (We have more or less inadvertently given banks the power to create new money more or less surreptitiously.) [See page 313.]

88. Corollary B: The Federal Reserve (The power of banks to create money has led to a government takeover of them, which is used for government's own surreptitious purposes.) [See page 314.]

89. Corollary C: Fed as Price Fixer (Everything the Fed does represents an effort to fix some of our most important economy-wide prices.) [See page 315.]

90. Corollary D: Reform (Banking can be put on a more solid foundation, most obviously by eliminating fractional reserve banking.) [See page 317.]

91. Corollary E: Bank Privatization (Money and banking services are not inherently different from other commercial services.) [See page 318.]

Laws of Government-Controlled Banking (Chapter XVI)

92. Law of Government-Controlled Banking: If we allow government to continue to tighten its control of banking, we should not be surprised if government uses this control for its own purposes, not to improve prospects for the economy. [See page 321.]

93. Corollary A: Government Financing Options 101 (In the end, the public pays one way or the other.) [See page 325.]

Laws of Spending Versus Saving (Chapter XVII)

94. Law of Spending Versus Saving: No one is so foolish as to try to spend his or her way to wealth. We create wealth by abstaining from spending, by saving, by making wise investments, and by working hard to make the investments as productive as possible. Governments are not exempt from this reality. Whether financed by taxes, debt, or money creation, its spending does not "stimulate" an economy. [See page 327.]

95. Corollary A: "Fiscal Stimulus" (Also Referred to as "Growth" Policy) [See page 329.]

96. Corollary B: Keynesian Financing "Tricks" (Borrowing is cheaper but more destructive if interest rates are controlled and especially if government borrows from itself.) [See page 333.]

Law of the Non-Neutrality of Money (Chapter XVIII)

97. Law of the Non-Neutrality of Money: Injecting new money into the economy from any source, whether fractional reserve banking, "quantitative easing," or "fiscal stimulus," by definition cannot be neutral, contrary to assertions in most economic textbooks. Non-neutrality of money matters a great deal for an economy. [See page 337.]

Law of the Non-Neutrality of Money, Newly Created Money, "Business Cycles," and Depressions (Chapter XIX)

98. Law of the Non-Neutrality of Money, Newly Created Money, "Business Cycles," and Depressions: The most fundamental source of chronic economic bubble and bust. [See page 341.]

Summary Laws of Economics (Chapter XX)

99. Summary Law of Economics: If you want a thriving economy, protect free and flexible prices. [See page 349.]

100. Corollary A: The test that distinguishes good government law pertaining to the economy from bad is that good government law does not interfere with, manipulate, or control prices. [See page 351.]

Endnotes

1. Ludwig von Mises, *Human Action: The Scholar's Edition* (Auburn, AL: Mises Institute, 2008) p. 2.

2. Ludwig von Mises, *Human Action: A Treatise on Economics* (Chicago: Henry Regnery Company, 1966), Chapter 2, Section 2.

3. Ibid., Chapter 2, Section 3.

4. Ibid., Chapter 2, Section 10.

5. Ibid., Chapter 3, Section 6.

6. *Weekly Standard* (February 2, 2009): 15.

7. David Hume, Essay "Of Interest."

8. *Grant's Interest Rate Observer* (September 16, 2016): 1.

9. Robby Soave, http://www.reason.com (October 14, 2016).

10. Richard Cowan, "How the Narcs Created Crack: A War Against Ourselves," *National Review* (December 5, 1986) 38 (23): 26–34

11. Mark Thornton, "Alcohol Prohibition Was a Failure" (July 17, 1991), Policy Analysis, http://www.Cato.org.

12. http://www.redstate.com (September 16, 2016).

13. To check the math, see Thomas Sowell, *Basic Economics: A Citizen's Guide to the Economy* (New York: Basic Books, 2000), 272-74.

14. David Hume, Essay "Of the Balance of Trade."

15. Merton Miller, *Institutional Investor* (September 1995): 59.

16. Paul McCulley, "Pacific Investment Management," *Fed Focus* (December 11, 2003): 4.

17. Friedrich A. Hayek, "The Use of Knowledge in Society," *American Economic Review*, 35:4 (September 1945): 519–30.

18. Friedrich A. Hayek, "The Use of Knowledge in Society," American Economic Review, 35:4 (September 1945): 519–30. Reprinted in Friedrich A. Hayek, *Individualism and Economic Order* (Chicago: Henry Regnery Company, 1972), 77–91.

19. Adam Smith, *The Wealth of Nations* (London, 1776), Book 4, Chapter 2.

20. Matt Ridley, *Genome* (New York: Harper Collins, 2000): 151.

21. Milton Friedman, *Capitalism and Freedom* (Chicago: University of Chicago Press, 1962), 129.

22. *Economist* (September 28, 1996): 28.

23. Paul Johnson, *Will Capitalism Survive* (Washington, DC: Ethics and Public Policy Center, 1979), 4; also in Michael Novak, *The Spirit of Democratic Capitalism* (New York: Madison Books, 1982), 121

24. Wilhelm Röpke, *Economics of the Free Society* (Chicago: Henry Regnery Company, 1963), 235.

25. Hunter Lewis, *Where Keynes Went Wrong: And Why World Governments Keep Creating Inflation, Bubbles, and Busts* (Mt. Jackson, VA: Axios Press, 2011), Note QQ, 331.

26. Walter Lippmann, *Interpretations: 1931–1932* (New York: Macmillan, 1932), 103-5.

27. John Maynard Keynes, *The General Theory of Employment, Interest, and Money* (London: Macmillan, 1936), 264, 267.

28. Lewis, *Where Keynes Went Wrong*, Note II, 326-

29. Henry Hazlitt, *Economics in One Lesson* (San Francisco: Laissez Faire Books, 1996), Part Two, Chapter 3.

30. Hunter Lewis, *Are the Rich Necessary? Great Economic Arguments and How They Reflect Our Personal Values, Updated & Expanded Edition* (Mt. Jackson, VA: Axios Press, 2009), 140.

31. Lewis, *Where Keynes Went Wrong*, 232.

32. Milton and Rose Friedman, *Free to Choose: A Personal Statement* (New York: Avon, 1981), 137.

33. http://www.healthblog.ncpa.org, Health Alerts (January 13, 2014).

34. *Forbes* (May 31, 2016): 112.

35. http://www.umcommission.org, John Wesley, "The Use of Money."

36. *Homeopathy Today* (Winter 2015): 23

37. *Grant's Interest Rate Observer* (October 14, 2016): 5.

38. Joseph Alsop, *I've Seen the Best of It* (New York: W. W. Norton, 1992), 473.

39. P. T. Bauer, *Equality, the Third World, and Economic Delusion* (Cambridge, MA: Harvard University Press, 1981), 9.

40. Mises, *Human Action*, Chapter VIII.

41. Charles Krauthammer, http://www.nydailynews.com (November 15, 2016).

42. Mises, *Human Action*, 721.

43. Ibid., Chapter XVI, Section 15.

44. Alexander Hamilton, Report to the House of Representatives, December 13, 1790, in American State Papers, Finance, 1st Congress, 3rd Session, no. 18, I, 67–76; also quoted in Jude Wanniski, *The Way the World Works: How Economies Fail—and Succeed* (New York: Basic Books, 1978), 204–5

45. Lewis, *Are the Rich Necessary?*, 132-133.

46. *New Yorker* (May 14, 2015): 30.

47. Röpke, *Economics of the Free Society*, 219; also in Randall Holcombe, *15 Great Austrian Economists* (Auburn, AL: Ludwig von Mises Institute, 1999), 215.

48. Donald T. Campbell, "Assessing the impact of planned social change." p. 85; *Evaluation and Program Planning,* 2(1): 67-90.

49. Franco Modigliani, "Liquidity, Preference, and the Theory of Interests, and Money," *Econometrica* (January 1944), 45-88.

50. *Weekly Standard* (February 1, 2009): 9; and *Washington Times* (March 9, 2009): 4.

51. Milton Friedman, in Wood, *Explorations in Economics Liberalism,* 17 and elsewhere.

52. Friedman, *Free to Choose,* 258.

53. Lewis, *Are the Rich Necessary?*, 243-248.

54. John Maynard Keynes, *The Economic Consequences of the Peace* (London, 1920), 236.

55. Murray Rothbard, *The Case Against the Fed* (Auburn, AL: Ludwig von Mises Institute, 1994), 42.

56. Martin Wolf, https://www.ft.com/content/50c73da8-bf6c-11de-a696-00144feab49a *(October 23, 2009).*

57. Keynes, "Economic Possibilities for Our Grandchildren," in *Essays in Persuasion,* 370.

58. Robert Skidelsky, *John Maynard Keynes* (London: Macmillan, 2000), vol. 2, 62.

59. Lewis, *Where Keynes Went Wrong*, 120.

60. John Maynard Keynes, *Collected Writings*, vol. 21, p. 326; and *The General Theory*, 127.

61. Lewis, *Where Keynes Went Wrong*, Note WW, 333-334.

62. *Weekly Standard* (April 13-20, 2009): 8.

63. David Hume, Essay "Of Public Credit."

64. Wartime radio broadcast, quoted in "The Commanding Heights," Yergin, et al, PBS.

65. Keynes, *The General Theory*, 235.

66. Ibid., 82-83.

67. *The Commercial and Financial Chronicle* (November 21, 1957), quoted in James Grant, *The Trouble with Prosperity: The Loss of Fear, the Rise of Speculation, and the Risk to American Savings* (New York: Random House, 1996), 37-38; also in Hunter Lewis, *How Much Money Does An Economy Need?* (Mt. Jackson, VA: Axios Press, 2007), 19.

68. Keynes, *The General Theory*, 220.

69. Friedrich A. Hayek, *Monetary Theory and the Trade Cycle* (London: Jonathan Cape, 1933), 21-22.

70. Keynes, *The General Theory*, 383.

71. David Hume, Essay "Of the Balance of Trade."

72. David Hume, Essay "Of Money."

73. John Maynard Keynes, *Collected Writings*, vol. 5, *A Treatise on Money: The Pure Theory of Money* (London: Macmillan; New York: St. Martin's Press, 1971), 83-84.

74. Hazlitt, *Economics in One Lesson*, Chapter 22, 151-157.

75. Keynes, *The Economic Consequences of the Peace*, 236.

76. John Stuart Mill, "Of the Influence of Production on Consumption," in *Essays on Some Unsettled Questions*

of Political Economy (London, 1844; actually written 1829-1830); also cited in Hazlitt, *Failure of the "New Economics,"* 366.

77. *Grant's Interest Rate Observer*, Brainerd Speech in Chicago (September 16, 2016): 1.

78. Thomas Macaulay, *History of England* (1848), Vol. 1, Chap. 3; quoted in Hazlitt, *Economics in One Lesson*, 15.

Index:
Economics in Three Lessons

Index:
One Hundred
Economic Laws